Cemetery 104

is dedicated to

Kurt Kahofer, who passed away shortly after the the completion of the restoration of the Schenck Family Burying Ground, Convent Road, Syosset, New York. And to the 48 Schenck Family members, Garrett Nostrand, and the other unknown souls at rest there.

Cemetery 104

AN EARLY AMERICAN BURYING GROUND LOST AND FOUND

RAV FREIDEL

TAPHOPHILE PRESS

The subject matter was an all-volunteer effort. Not a scientific reconstruction.

ISBN 979-8-218-84187-4
Rav@agencyrav.com

Praise and admiration goes to the Burying Ground Preservation Group
for preserving American history. 2018–2023

Table of Contents

Foreword

It is in the nature of repairing and preserving historic cemeteries, whether for deciphering epitaphs encrusted with lichens or for reattaching broken stones, that unforeseen conditions arise at every turn. But the Schenck Cemetery is in a class of its own.

When Rav Freidel introduced us to the site in fall 2018, we sensed a formidable challenge and one without an obvious outcome. What sense could be made of the hundreds of stone fragments scattered across the site? Could any of these grave markers be reassembled and reerected? What explained the desecration?

The "we" is the Burying Ground Preservation Group, Inc., a nonprofit that Kurt E. Kahofer and I formed in early retirement. Our purpose is to document and preserve historic cemeteries and to create public programs that encourage appreciation and awareness. We're joined in our work by Joel C. Snodgrass, a stone conservator and fellow graduate of Columbia University's Program in Historic Preservation.

We share a passion for preserving old cemeteries and have worked successfully at numerous sites across Long Island. Nothing, however, prepared us for the Schenck Cemetery.

If it weren't for Rav's unrelenting determination, single-minded devotion, and belief in the "rightness" of the mission, our work wouldn't have started. Included in Town historian John Hammond's *Historic Cemeteries of Oyster Bay* (2007), the Schenck Cemetery is one of many Colonial-era burying grounds created by families then living in semi-isolation away from distant settlements.

With the passing of time and suburbanization, however, these vest pocket "parks" are under increasing threat. After purchasing the early-eighteenth-century Dutch-framed Schenck-Mann House across Convent Road, Rav discovered that the historic family cemetery survived. Determined to save it from oblivion, he contacted us.

It goes without saying that working with Rav to reclaim and restore the Schenck Cemetery has been one of the most rewarding experiences of our work in historic cemeteries. Devising ways of gridding the site to record and excavate stone fragments, collecting pieces to match lettering and shapes, and assembling stones for reattachment and resetting has enabled us to resurrect much that remains of the Schenck Cemetery.

And it was all possible because of Rav's vision. The Town of Oyster Bay is richer for that.

–Zachary N. Studenroth

INTRODUCTION

My wife calls me 'Tombstone'

I suppose there are worse things she could call me. Fortunately, it's not "My ex." Although I do give her reasons.

When we go for a walk, Sandy won't hold my hand, because I have a habit of picking up trash. Virtually anyplace you can think of is somebody's garbage can, and the filth offends me. So I carry a bag, get in some much-needed exercise, and pick it up. It's the one revolting human behavior I can actually do something about. I feel better, and everybody benefits.

Then there's training seven days a week, three to four months a year, to go off hiking in the Grand Canyon. At which time I give up drinking and smoking weed. I'm wound much too tight. My behavior crosses the line to godawful. And even I don't like my crotchety self.

And of course there are the usual misdemeanors—shouting, talking to myself (and the cat), and the occasional gastrointestinal distress.

But what Sandy finds most off-putting is the subject of this book. For the past several years, I've been completely obsessed with putting together the greatest jigsaw puzzle of my life. One that's lifesize and made of broken stones.

I'm the official caretaker of the Schenck Family Burying Ground in the Hamlet of Syosset, Town of Oyster Bay, New York. Sometimes life gives you the chance to right a terrible wrong. I've enriched mine by taking that chance.

"Help the Ukrainians!" she says. "They're getting a lot of help," I tell her. "No one else gives a rat's patootie about this!" But maybe you will.

And by the way, I do help the Ukrainians. I drink their vodka.

CHAPTER 1

A family in mourning

June 27, 1804: East Woods, New York

There was no first name. No initial. No year. Carved into what was left of this busted-up fieldstone was the surname—Schenck. When Zach Studenroth first pointed it out to me, in late 2018, he saw a date, June 27. Three years into the restoration, I found the year 1804 buried below grade. This was the oldest engraved headstone in the Schenck Family Burying Ground located 300 yards behind the farmhouse I live in today.

That date, June 27, 1804, does not exist on any of the lists of the deceased at the site, called surveys, with the earliest recorded in 1902. So, who was this person whom family and friends grieved over, and who were the Schencks? This is where the story begins.

Schenck is a Dutch and German name for a trade, like Carpenter or Taylor or Mason. It means cup bearer, wine pourer, or innkeeper. You pronounce it *Skenk*.

According to local historian Tom Montalbano, the Schenck family were pioneers who came to East Woods in the late 1600s and built their house sometime between 1680 and 1710. It's in the northeast corner of Oyster Bay Town, renamed Syosset in 1854. Their 97-acre farm was purchased from a group in Rhode Island that had bought it from an Englishman named Robert Williams. Williams had bartered for it in 1648 from the Matinecock Indians for a few dollars' worth of cloth. The farm extended about a mile east and west on today's Convent Road, and north to the Syosset-Woodbury railroad crossing. Their yield was buckwheat, potatoes, corn, beans, squash, cabbage, cucumbers, and meats/dairy.

In colonial times, there was a handful of farmsteads in this mostly oak and pine forest. Today it's the burbs: 18,800 residents according to the 2022 census. And very few have ever heard the name Schenck. Other than that, I could find very little written about them.

The restored June 27, 1804, marker. Notice the similar break in the fieldstone in the foreground.

Author's note: The front of each headstone faces west.

As luck would have it, nearly five years after the start of piecing together their cemetery, I entered the right combination of words in a Google search, and up came *A Documented History of the Dutch Congregation of Oyster Bay, Island of Nassau, Now Long Island* by Henry A. Stoutenbergh.

I'm about to go biblical on you, so fasten your seatbelt. The genealogy is challenging. Published in 1900, it contains Dutch Reformed Church records for virtually every male in the Schenck Family Burying Ground. Along with the names are their names and the dates when they were born (b.), were baptized (bp.), died, and were buried (bd.). It also includes spouses' (m.) and children's names (Issue). And in some cases, the Last Will and Testament.

Arranged alphabetically, on page 474, is the following:

John Schenck, of O.B.,[1] *Son of John and Maragritye Hegeman, b. Sep. 29, 1750; d. June 27, 1804; bd. June 28, 1804: m., May 20, 1773, Sarah Van Nostrand, dau. of Aaron and Wainche Luyster, b. Sep. 28. 1753; bp. Mch. 12, 1754, at W.H.*[2] *(witnesses, Peter Luyster and Sarah Monfoort); d. April 22, 1808; bd. April 24, 1808. (From a Bible record in possession of Phebe S. Foster.)*

Issue:

John, m. Mary Hegeman
Wainche, b. Friday, Nov. 3, 1780; bp. Mch. 18, 1781; d. Mch. 28, 1830
Aaron, m. Sarah Bennet
Moses, b. Wednesday, Dec. 16, 1789; bp. Mch. 21, 1790
Maragriet, b. Friday, July 4, 1794; bp. Aug. 17, 1794

There it was: "**d. June 27, 1804.**" Henry Stoutenbergh's book made the unknown known. We now had a first name, John.

And one gravesite over from John's engraved marker, which is among the oldest in the cemetery, is most likely that of Sarah, his wife. The modest marble stone that is there now has blurred scripture and is missing the top, where her name, death, and birthdate would be. The restoration team was able to decipher the text: "Behold my mother/My brothers be resigned/Tho far from you, I must/And home you'll comfort find."

[1] Oyster Bay

[2] Wolver Hollow, now Brookville, is the site of the Reformed Dutch Church of Oyster Bay, built in 1734.

Since so much has been pulled out of the ground and moved around at the site, it is equally plausible that Sarah's headstone is among one of the surrounding fieldstones. Which I believe is more likely. She died just four years after her husband. However, if it is in fact her marker, it's probably the first marble stone set in the family cemetery.

Which made me wonder why her name wasn't recorded on any survey either. Nor were the names of John's parents, John Schenck and Maragritye Hegeman.[3]

According to Stoutenbergh's book, John's father is resting there, too: He was born in Flatlands, Brooklyn on May 23, 1718, and died December 15, 1775. "He settled in East Woods (Syossset). The burying yard is located on the farm."

That makes John's father perhaps the first to be buried at the cemetery and, without doubt, the builder of the Schenck farmhouse. The oldest timbers date back to 1734, according to a dendrochronology report. And Stoutenbergh confirms it by writing that his grandfather Stephen Janse Schenck (b. January 2, 1680, d. November 6, 1767) left a will making a bequest to his son, "to pay for the plantation of land he now lives on at O.B. in Queens Co." This places the Schenck family arrival in the late 1720s, early 1730s. Not the late 1600s as the local historian had written. According to a 1732 document, John's father was one of the founders of the first Dutch Reformed Church in nearby Wolver Hollow, now called Brookville. My guess is he was either living on the land and clearing it for farming or staying at one of the nearby farms before building his house in 1734.

And Stoutenbergh writes that John's mother, Maragritye, was born in 1719. No date is given for her death. It's safe to assume she is in perpetual repose next to her husband. No one will ever know which of the shattered fieldstone markers belonged to them. Or their children, including Adrian (d. 1777) and Nicklaes (d. 1796), as well as their spouses, Neltje Bennet and Sytie Emons.

At the urging of an old friend and member of the Dutch Colonial Society, I typed in "John Schenck, June 27, 1804" on Google. It led me to his genealogy. His family history dates back a thousand years to Edgar de Schenken, born in Germany before the year 816. And John's father was christened Jan Stevense Schenck. Not John. Jan is pronounced Yăn," which sounds like "John."

[3] Listed as Margarieta Adriaense Hageman on FamilySearch.org. Apparently spelling standards didn't exist. Different spellings are the rule for virtually every Dutch forename and surname.

And the great-grandfather of the John Schenck whom this chapter is all about is Jan Martense Schenck (1632 maybe 1636–1689). Jan Martense along with his sister Annetje and brother Roelof were the first people named Schenck to come to the colonies. They arrived in New Amsterdam from Holland among 140 passengers on June 28, 1650, aboard De Valckenier (the Falconer). They settled in a farming area the English would rename Flatlands, Brooklyn. Jan Martense partnered in a tidal grist mill. Today it's known as Mill Basin.

And here's the best part. Jan Martense's house still stands today. It is the second-oldest house in the State of New York. He built it in 1676. It was dismantled in 1952 and rebuilt in 1960. If you would like to see it, visit the fourth floor of the Brooklyn Museum!

Finally, John Schenck and his wife are a few graves from their son John, born in 1774; and his wife, Mary, born the year before him; and another son, Aaron, who was born in 1773 or 1774 (headstone indicates the former, church records the latter).

Aaron's beaten and battered marble marker was reassembled from 15 unearthed elements. There are still pieces missing. And sandwiched between Aaron and his mother and father is Aaron's wife. Also named Sarah. Her marble headstone has been almost completely restored. Aaron and Sarah had no children. Yet next to Aaron's marker is another Aaron. As I said, somebody was playing something akin to musical chairs with the headstones.

But I'm way too deep in the weeds and getting much too far ahead of myself.

Aaron Schenck (November 7, 1783 –October 17,1871), second son of John Schenck.

Zach Studenroth first spotted the inscription "Schenck June 27" chiseled in the broken rock. The small heart-shaped piece was found nearby.

Possibly Sarah Van Nostrand, wife of second-generation East Woods farmer John Schenck.

The ragtag remains of the back row. From left to right: Aaron; a second Aaron; Sarah, wife of Aaron; Aaron's mother and father, Sarah and the John who died June 27, 1804; Emma Jane Wanser; John's first son, also named John; and his wife, Mary. Catharine Baldwin is last.

CHAPTER 2

An invitation to a cemetery tour. Oh boy!

Nobody will confuse me with an ichthyologist. Although I do have the contact information for some of the foremost shark scientists in the world on my cell phone. One of the hats I wear is being "shark hugger in residence" where I spend most of my time: Montauk, New York. Until recently this is where sharks were killed for prize money, not food. Which wouldn't be a problem if they weren't being slaughtered beyond sustainability to satisfy the demand for shark fin soup in the Asian market.

In early September 2018, I was heading to Silver Spring, Maryland, to attend a Highly Migratory Species meeting conducted by the National Marine Fisheries Service (a branch of the National Oceanic and Atmospheric Administration). Just before I left, the artist, environmental activist, and my shark-saving comrade-in-arms April Gornik sent me an email inviting me to visit one of the oldest cemeteries in historic Sag Harbor, where she lives.

A couple of historians were planning to show off their restoration work, which included the graves of Revolutionary War veterans.

I wanted to go. Not so much to see the cemetery, which wasn't exactly my idea of a good time, but to meet the restorers. I had no idea people did this sort of thing. I sent April my regrets, explaining where I was headed, and asked her to get their contact information—telling her that I owned an old farmhouse in Syosset that predated the country and that associated with the house was a cemetery badly in need of restoration.

Upon my return, April had introduced me via email to Zach Studenroth. Our first communication was September 20, 2018.

About a month later, Zach, his associate Kurt Kahofer, and I met for the first time. I showed them the house, which they knew much more about than I did. Then we crossed the street, entered property owned by the Catholic Church, walked up a long driveway, climbed a hill, and toured the overgrown tree- and brush-covered burying ground.

They saw broken dark gray marble chunks lying all over the place and were aghast. Kurt said, "We've never seen anything like this!" Some of it was so far gone that it was literally a pile of mush—like melted sugar cubes. Once in a while, Zach would try to read an inscription from a fragment. He said the marble isn't dirty, it's covered with lichens and other plant growth that can be cleaned with a nontoxic solution. "We should be able to read the writing again."

There were several broken pedestal bases with no sign of the headstones. "An inferior design," Zach said. He explained that by using a big base for the headstone to slide into, tongue-and-groove style, the memorial masons saved marble. However, where the base and headstone join, they often broke.

Near the northeast corner of the site, there was one seriously eroded broken brownstone monument next to a smashed fieldstone. Behind those and to the right, jutting a few inches up from the ground, and broken, of course, was the inscribed "Schenck June 27" fieldstone. Which Zach noticed and said is very rare.

He told me, "Fieldstones were for people who couldn't afford marble. It's unusual to find one engraved." Zach and Kurt's knowledge left my head spinning. Off the main burial mound, to the east, they showed me more fieldstones lying flat on the earth. There were nearly 20 of them. Zach explained that they were most likely markers for people important to the family, such as "hired hands, nannies, and slaves."

How ironic, I thought. They were important but not worthy of lying side by side with the Schencks. Yet nobody was worthy of being spared the total desecration of this place. It wasn't a cemetery. It was a crime scene. Kurt remembered my saying, "This isn't right. Something has to be done. It needs your help."

Before leaving, Zach said, "One other person has to look at the site before we would consider taking it on." Adding, "It is the best-kept secret on Long Island!"

The burying yard after the debris was removed, January 2019.

CHAPTER 3

Waiting for Joel

It would be a two-month wait.

Email, October 17, 2018:

Good evening Rav: Kurt and I enjoyed meeting you today and getting a tour of your house as well as the nearby burying ground. The house and its surrounding landscape are remarkable survivors in an area that has become so built up.

We're going to discuss optional treatments for the burying ground with our colleague, Joel Snodgrass, whose specialty is stone conservation. There are several monuments that appear eligible for restoration; others have weathered to the point of total loss. But through research, we may find information that helps to inform both the restoration and possible signage that could identify those buried there whose markers are illegible. Best regards, Zach

Email, October 30, 2018:

We hope to have a proposal for you after your trip out West.[4] Essential to the assessment and calculation of the scope is for our third partner and stone conservator, Joel Snodgrass, to walk the site and make his own observations. Although the focus is on reassembling the headstones that are best preserved, the issue of how to record and stabilize the many fragments scattered across the site remains.

This may require developing a methodology for the site which is not that uncommon, but rarely encountered to this extent. We're looking forward to the challenge!

Email, December 15, 2018:

...I'm emailing you and copying Joel Snodgrass, our colleague and stone conservator, who could undertake the restoration in the Schenck Family Burying Ground. Joel visited the site, but was unable to clear it sufficiently

[4] Grand Canyon hike

of leaves to get a good look at what's lying on the ground and eligible for repair.

At this point, I suggest that you & Joel meet at the site to discuss the scope. Kurt & I are ready to jump in and do what's necessary to clean, record, photograph and upload the inscriptions to the internet, if these are agreed to be part of the job, but deciding on the number of stones that can be re-erected is key to understanding the scope of this project.

Later that day, Joel and I arranged to meet at 1 p.m. on Tuesday, December 18. Ever onward, I thought. Then overnight I had an epiphany. In the morning, I dashed off the following:

Morning guys, ... So as not to waste your time, should I approach the Church and tell them what we would like to do?

Zach's reply:

Realizing that getting approval from the Church may take time, I agree that approaching them soon is a good idea.

Very little work actually happens at a site during the winter months, therefore developing the scope can happen simultaneously with securing permission to do the project. You may find that the administrators of either Our Lady of Mercy Academy or Mercy First can grant permission, but as Church-owned property, this may not be the case.

If any questions arise, please feel free to forward them to us for clarification as to the nature of the work and its historical significance and benefit to the community.

I was fretting about the unresolved issue of getting permission from the Church. Suppose they remembered me as one of the obstacles to their development plans 15 years earlier? Which I'd better address now.

In 2002 we had been living in the countryside setting for two and a half years while Sandy was recovering from breast cancer surgery and chemotherapy, followed by radiation. Meanwhile, the Church was embroiled in a child abuse scandal and needed to raise money to pay off victims of lecherous priests. We got a tip from the New York State Department of Transportation (which had designs on the woodlands bordering our land) that the Church was moving full speed ahead to turn the 40 rural acres to our east into a massive privately run nursing home. When they were finished, there wouldn't be a blade of grass left.

In the past, I've locked horns with the US Environmental Protection Agency, the US Navy, the US Army Corps of Engineers, the Connecticut Department of Energy and Environmental Protection, the New York State Department of Conservation, as well as a whole host of developers. However, stopping the Catholic Church was a much different story. They have God on their side. For Sandy and me to stand a chance of defeating the Archdiocese of Rockville Center, I knew we would need the help of a powerhouse New York City law firm.

An attorney friend recommended Stephen Cass, a partner at the Wall Street law firm of Carter, Ledyard, Milburn (established 1854, the same year East Woods had its name changed to Syosset). Stephen is the environmental lawyer who stopped Westway from being built over the Hudson River.

Stephen said he would have to check to find out if there were any conflicts of interest preventing us from retaining his services. If not, his bill would be $200,000!

There was no way we could afford that. So, he suggested that for $20,000 he would fire a bunch of warning shots across the Church's bow. His plan was to bombard them with letters, and hopefully they would back off, or at least scale back their plans. It was a bluff I was willing to make.

While Stephen did a title search, he asked me to find any local civic groups that would be opposed to the development and locate any documents I could find relating to the land in question. First, Sandy and I contacted Citizens for a More Beautiful Syosset, who met at our house, and then Ron Burckley, the man we'd bought the house from.

The Syosset group was adamant that they wanted the Church property left alone. This was the only green space left in the Hamlet. Their attorney said he would contact the Church to let them know they were in for a fight. Ron lent us a 1947 survey of our property that he still had in his possession. He said, "They can't do it." Written on the land where the nursing home would go was the reason: "Land of Sisters of Mercy Convent (Set Aside in Perpetuity for Park Purposes)." The survey, prepared by Louis W. Waters, was guaranteed by the Title Guarantee and Trust Company, New York City.

By the winter of 2003, the Church, sensing opposition to the nursing home, rented out a banquet hall and held a meeting to gauge public sentiment toward the project. Approximately 200 Syosset citizens showed up. For every 10 speakers,

9 were opposed. Soon afterwards, the Church folded its tent and withdrew its application. We were safe. For the time being.

Another two weeks passed, and Stephen Cass's associate finally called me to report on the title search. "Are you ready? All the files are gone!" Nobody had any records on the land. They had vanished into thin air. Not a trace. Missing. Kaput. "Oh, my God!" I said, "The power of the Church!" They had somehow been able to reach into the drawers of the Town and Nassau County clerks' offices and remove the documents.

Sandy called Ron Burckley to return his survey. When he stopped by the house, he asked me if I'd ever seen the cemetery. "What cemetery?" I asked. And he took me for a walk across the street onto the Church property.

I felt like guns were pointed at me as we walked up the driveway. To our right was a long two-story building, to our left a parking lot surrounded by a large field with trees behind that. As we continued along, I saw a sign identifying the building—the Thomas F. Casey Center—which appeared to be offices connecting to a meeting hall or a dining room. Continuing north, passing a "Do not enter" sign and a series of dumpsters, we reached a steep grass incline. Up the hill at the highest point of land on the right, hidden in the trees and dense foliage, were a dozen or so stone nubs in addition to stone fragments scattered across the branch- and leaf-covered ground. I could see writing on some of the broken pieces but nothing legible. I couldn't even tell that it was once a cemetery. We walked around together for a few minutes, and then I escorted him to his car and soon forgot about the graveyard.

In order to get permission from the Church to restore the cemetery, I decided to approach the one person I knew who worked there. His name was Mark. Whenever it snowed, even though I had somebody plow our driveway (which in olden days was a road, and before that an Indian trail), the Highway Department's snowplows would block us in again. I'd grab my snow shovel and try to dig us out, and Mark, who drove a small snowplow to clear the Church property, would invariably see me and ask if I needed help. I'd generally have it under control, unless it was a monster snowstorm or wet, heavy slush and ice. In such a case, I'd accept his offer. When he was finished, I'd smile, put my hands together, bow graciously, and ask him what kind of wine he liked to drink. He'd always refuse the wine. "Well, what *do* you drink?" I finally asked. He responded, "Tea. Lipton tea." So off I went to the supermarket to buy a box of tea and then walked up the driveway where he'd parked his plow and left it on the driver's seat with a note of thanks.

Since Mark was my one connection to the Church, I decided I would ask him for guidance on how to get permission to restore the cemetery—after Joel examined it, of course. For all I knew, he'd recommend turning down the job.

As to Joel, he was waiting for me at the appointed hour. He had parked in the Church lot. I arrived with my rake in hand, and while we walked and talked, I put it to work. He was photographing the broken marble I kept exposing. Even I was surprised by how much there was—all shapes and sizes. Places nowhere near the graves had fragments. Some with writing, others not. There was so much leaf litter to remove and no way for me to rake it all up in his presence.

Joel explained that he does restoration work at many cemeteries. I assumed he was quite religious and that this was a calling for him. He said he had never seen so much damage. I asked him what it would cost to fix it. He didn't answer. "$10,000? … $20,000? … $100,000?" "Not that much," he said.

After half an hour, he told me he would talk to the others and get back to me. I had my doubts that I'd ever see him again.

That night there was an email from Joel in my inbox:

Hello Rav, It was nice to meet you at the Schenck-Mann[5] Burying Ground this afternoon and review conditions together. I was encouraged to see there are far more cases of potential restoration than I originally believed, and that much of the burial markers appear to survive, although in many cases as broken elements. Given the complexity that exists, I thought it might be helpful to briefly review the main points of our overview and assumed next steps:

As noted, in order to generate accurate information regarding specific treatments, as well as extent and from that a cost proposal, it is necessary to be able to see the stones clearly so that actual conditions can be fully assessed and quantified. However, given the current state with heavy leaf coverage, it's not really possible to do so at this time.

- *Given that, I think it makes the most sense that the site is first cleared via a "spring clean-up" approach, although I understand that you intend to carry out that process during the winter months. That would be fine, as it would then allow a follow-up visit to review the stones more closely.*

[5] George Mann was the next owner of the Schenck family farm.

- *Once cleared we can fully examine all the conditions to allow an estimate based on the steps and materials required in each case, and following that, a proposal can be generated.*
- *I also think your suggestion is wise to reach out to church staff contacts you already have, in order to begin discussing the possibility of carrying out work at the site and getting permission to do so.*
- *In the interim, we'll put our thoughts to possible funding sources that might consider supporting such a project. I fully understand the likelihood that the Church will not want any publicity or attention drawn to the site, which I'm sure we can avoid.*

Thus, if you could let us know when the site will be cleared (no rush, it's getting cold out there!), we can then schedule another review and go from there... have a great holiday!

CHAPTER 4

Whose land is this, anyway?

It was early Sunday morning one day before the start of 2019. I noticed Mark's plow off in the distance, parked up the driveway near his office. The parking lot was empty, except for a few white vans with the Mercy First name and logo.

I walked past the plow and knocked on his heavy steel door. It was so thick that I needed to rap on it again with my house keys. A moment passed, and Mark peeked out. He opened the door wider, smiled, invited me inside, and asked me to sit down.

The room was small. His desk and surroundings cluttered. A picture window was behind him for an adjoining office. Mark had a computer on his desk and all kinds of objects on the shelves filled to capacity—hats, cups, tools, photos. My eyes were fixed on him, though. He looked to be in his late 70s. About my height. Had a flat-top haircut. Like a Marine.

I told him I'd lived in the old farmhouse for the last 20 years and wanted to take a crack at restoring the cemetery on the Church property—mentioning that some of the people who were buried there had lived in my house. I asked him if he would introduce me to the powers that be, so I could get their okay.

Much to my surprise, he said I needed to talk to the Town Parks Department. They take care of the cemetery. Not the Church. I slumped back in the chair, but inside my head, I was doing cartwheels.

Mark said that he had been at his job for more than 40 years. He gave me his business card: Mark Kurnicki, Director of Maintenance, Mercy First. There were his email address and cell phone number.

He explained that in 1893, the Schenck family had sold land to the Sisters of Mercy. A deal was reached with the Town to rename the street Convent Road and extend it about half a mile to the east, and in exchange the Town would care for the Schenck cemetery. What he told me, I took as gospel. Something I would later regret.

"A woeful job they did." I said to him. "The place is a disaster."

Mark gave me the contact information for his boss and the phone number for the Parks Department, which he didn't think very highly of. He was delighted with our visit and happy to hear that the cemetery might be fixed. Before I left, he said, "If you need anything, give me a call."

I couldn't believe my luck and relayed the news to Zach, Kurt, and Joel later that day.

Zach replied almost immediately:

...This is very interesting! In many ways it'll make working on the site (and getting permission) easier, although both the Town and the Church have their own bureaucratic obstacles.

The Oyster Bay historian has the site on his list. I wonder about access, because the site must be land locked, but I'm sure that can be worked out. Please keep us posted as you navigate Town Hall.

CHAPTER 5
Approaching the Town

What possesses people to do things so out of character? My nature has always been to speak up for the natural world. Fish can't speak, birds can't speak, trees can't speak. I'm happy to do it for them. Even if I'm not the most eloquent spokesman. The way I see it, adding another voice to the wilderness is better than there being no voice at all. But restoring a cemetery? For people I don't know? Who aren't related to me? And it's not even on my land. That's way beyond the pale.

If I were religious, that might be one thing. But I'm not the least bit religious. I don't even want to be buried. Cremate me, and throw my ashes in a garbage can. Or better yet, compost me. Maybe I can help make a tree grow.

Perhaps my motivation was guilt. The guilt of being lucky enough to born free in America. The guilt of a laundry list of bad decisions I wish I could walk back.

Perhaps it's the desire to still be relevant—to justify my existence—to try to make one last difference and leave the world a little better than I found it.

We'd done so much work on their farmhouse, pond, barn, and land. It seemed only right to save their burial ground, too. Funny thing is, I don't know whether the Schencks were good people or not. Were they slaveholders? Long Island had the largest population of enslaved people in the north. Oyster Bay had an official position called the "Negro whipper."

I suppose, like everybody else, some were good, some were bad, and some were in between. What I do know is this: They had hard, and often short, lives, and except for some obscure church records and a few surveys, those broken marble relics are the only record that these people ever existed. And if I didn't step in to save them, nobody else would. Somehow putting them back together became essential to me.

Given that it was the holiday, I waited until Thursday, January 3, to make my call to the Parks Department. The lady I spoke with had me on hold for a good five minutes. She was not familiar with the cemetery—in fact, nobody was. Oyster Bay is a big town. They mow lots of cemeteries, and it wasn't exactly mowing season. She suggested I call the Town supervisor's office, which I promptly did.

The supervisor's secretary heard me out and said I need to contact the Town historian. This was his bailiwick. She produced a phone number, and I left a message for John Hammond, who returned my call four days later.

I told John the same thing I'd told everyone else: I'd been living in the house for 20 years, got it on the National Register of Historic Places, restored the pond, and scraped and painted the circa-1890 barn—and now I wanted to fix the cemetery. When I told him about Zach and Kurt, whose last names I couldn't remember, he rattled them off. And I also mentioned a guy named Joel. "Joel Snodgrass," he said.

Hammond took down my email address and on January 8, sent me this:

As we discussed on the phone yesterday the Town of Oyster Bay has an Abandoned Cemetery Adoption Program. You had indicated that you were interested in adopting the Schenck Family Cemetery in Syosset. Attached is a Standard Letter of Indemnification which is required to move your request forward. The name of the contractor should be your organization or corporation.

I typed up an indemnification letter, which took the Town off the hook should an accident happen, and copied the Burying Ground Preservation Group. I asked myself, "What could go wrong?" Everything is already on the ground, or under it. I was off and running.

Then I emailed Hammond again:

I enjoyed speaking with you yesterday and I will mail the adoption paperwork shortly. Please tell me again how many abandoned cemeteries there are in Oyster Bay Town, the number was astonishing.

I was also wondering if there are any old photos or documents on the Schenck-Mann cemetery that might aid us in piecing together what goes where on the site? ... Is a historic restoration grant something that the Town could apply for?

He replied that there are about 126 cemeteries and that a little more than half are abandoned. This one was Cemetery 104. He had no photos other than those taken recently, had never seen a map or plot plans, and had no information about funding sources.

Hammond added:

...perhaps Zach and Joel have some info on grants; they did the restoration of the Baptist Church Cemetery in Oyster Bay a few years ago.

The Burying Ground Preservation Group, February 4, 2019: Joel Snodgrass, Zach Studenroth, and Kurt Kahofer.

One of many gravestones that Joel believed was smashed with a sledgehammer.

Exposing the white piece of marble revealed the top half of a buried headstone.

A few days later Zach contacted me:

That's great news that the burying ground is Town-owned and that Hammond can grant permission to work on it with a Letter of Indemnification. And although the site is landlocked, it's probably safe to assume the Church will agree to access across their parking lot, too.

We should now establish a scope of work, at least an initial one, which given the condition of the stones that are visible (and the possibility that there are others hidden below grade), might change as work proceeds. Cleaning and recording what's in evidence, and some strategic probes to determine if more fragments survive in the ground that match those that have fallen, is a logical place to start. Once we've determined the number of tablets that are eligible for repair, we can estimate the costs associated with those. My guess is 6 to 8 stones will fit this description.

With regard to funding, unless there is some demonstrated public benefit or educational purpose served by restoring the site, I'm not aware of any support it might receive. And as a Town-owned site, the costs associated with its repair are not tax-deductible. If the Oyster Bay Historical Society were willing to sponsor the work (or better still, "partner" with the Town Historian in launching a burying ground preservation project of some sort), the costs would be deductible (as a donation to the OBHS) and a foundation created for future work across the Town that could serve a public benefit...I suggest we meet sometime soon to explore these ideas.

It didn't take long for Hammond to approve the adoption, and I set my sights on getting rid of the fallen leaves for the restoration team. At first, I considered renting a leaf blower, but I detest those things. The noise could wake up the dead, and you could choke to death on the fumes.

Instead, I decided to work up a sweat and rake the leaves into manageable piles—hoping the Town would collect them. (They didn't.) In the process, I uncovered a few more large fragments and sent the images to Zach and company, as well as Hammond. Then, using my bow saw, I started cutting away the honeysuckle branches, small maple trees, low-hanging limbs, and the rest of the small overgrowth dominating the site. The big stuff would need a chainsaw.

I also wrote to Gerry McCaffery, the administrator of Mercy First, to let him know what was up. He wanted to know the size of Joel's trailer and get assurance that everything would be locked up at the end of the day, and I was to notify Mark when any of us crossed Church land to work on the site.

Zach, Kurt, and Joel set up a visit for January 31. On the 30th, it was 8 degrees and snowing. We pushed back the meeting until the following week.

Monday, February 4, 2019, with the leaves and tree limbs in prodigious piles, Zach, Kurt, Joel, and I all got together for the first time. They took a good look at what they would be working with.

During the raking, I'd uncovered many fragments we hadn't seen before. They were still in shock about what they were seeing. Kurt thought somebody had run over the graves with a truck. Joel thought they had been bashed to bits with a sledgehammer and pointed to examples scattered on the ground.

When they left, I continued cleaning up and cutting away the vegetation. Occasionally I'd spot something small and white, mostly hidden underground. Following Zach's instructions, I used a plastic trowel and my broom to remove what was around it. One that I thought was a small fragment, located in the northeast corner of the property, turned out to be so large that it looked to me like an entire gravestone. I took a photo and sent it to the team, and Joel said, "It was only a top half." But he was delighted to see it and figured there was much more. He hoped it would fit on one of the tabs sticking out of the ground.

A few days later, Kurt sent me an aerial photo of the parcel lines. I figured it was from a Town or Nassau County map. But it didn't look right to me. It was a triangle. With the hypotenuse going from southwest to northeast. And the right angle to the west. However, the Church treated the area like a square. Outside of the square, everything was mowed, clean, and manicured. Inside, it was a mess—with no shortage of marble scattered beyond the triangle.

CHAPTER 6

Making sense of it all

I had permission from the Town historian and the Church. I had a restoration team, although I didn't know how much they would cost. I had a lot of puzzle pieces strewn all over the place. And I had no idea what to do next.

I asked the preservation group to please contact the Town historian to try to get more cooperation from the Town for the preparation of the site. Kurt wrote to John Hammond, who, in turn, contacted the Parks Department to arrange a cleanup. However, the ground was too soft for trucks to drive up to the cemetery. Some of the tree limbs that had fallen were massive, and I couldn't move them myself. I would have to be patient.

As the weeks passed, every time I entered the property either to clear brush or look for buried stones, I contacted Mark, as I promised I would do, and continued to do so until he retired, in March 2024. He said he was happy I had taken on the project. I also contacted Ron Burckley, the former owner of the Schenck-Mann house. Ron was looking for old photos and anything else he could find to help with the project.

I thought, wouldn't it be great if he had a picture with everything to use as a guide? And shared my thoughts with the team. It would be a big help, was the obvious reply.

There was another place to look, the Syosset library. A librarian provided the phone number of the library historian, Barney Levantino, who was not in that day. When we finally spoke, he said he would try to find old church records to see who might be buried in what I was calling a cemetery and Zach was calling a burying ground.

There is a difference. Cemeteries are large, more numerous places that don't adhere to strict grave alignments. Burying grounds, sometimes referred to as graveyards or burying yards, tend to be smaller. Often associated with a church, or even smaller, such as a family site. This was that. With all the headstone inscriptions facing west. And footstones with initials facing east. The body laid between (with the head to the west).

Zach had explained that come the Resurrection on Judgment Day, all the dead would rise, facing the sunrise. (I should mention Zach was the former Southampton Town historian—the oldest English settlement in New York state.)

Barney Levantino wanted something in return for his help. He requested that I do a podcast on the old house for the library and the project I was undertaking, and he wanted the Burying Ground Preservation Group to do one, too. I said, yes, of course, I would and that I would check with Zach.

I was more than a bit confused by one thing, though, and—as it turned out—at least a dozen more. I thought the burying ground was Catholic, since the Schencks had sold their land to the Sisters of Mercy. Barney thought otherwise, and so did Zach. Dutch Reformed is what they said. Which, I would learn, is Protestant. Little did I know there was no love lost between the Catholics and the Protestants. Of course, if I weren't such a slow study, I would have realized that the Catholics would never have allowed their own graveyard to deteriorate into this condition. And had I done my due diligence, I would have visited the Sisters of Mercy website and learned that in 1893 they had bought their land from the Nostrands, not the Schencks.

Zach said he was not averse to publicity and would be happy to do a podcast. I let Barney know.

While I continued to search for as much information as I could find, a tennis partner of my wife's sent Sandy an email that she forwarded to me. It contained a link to *A Syosset Scrapbook*, which were historic photos of Syosset that I eagerly went through. It didn't take long to find a 1909 picture of our house with the farmer George Mann in the photo.

Next I found a photo of young Ron Burckley in the 1950s surrounded by other kids. The caption said: "The Burckley family for many years owned the old Schenck house on Convent Road, built c. 1680 to 1710. When the house and land were sold, the Burckley family stipulated that the house and barn be preserved and a lot of the surrounding land be kept from development. The house is now a Federal landmark."[6]

[6] There is no stipulation. Raymond Burckley tried to place the house on the National Register of Historic Places. It was rejected by New York State, because he had made modifications to the original design by adding dormers to the second floor. Today, the modifications, which are more than 50 years old, are historic, and the house was nominated for the National Register by the New York State Department of Parks Recreation and Historic Preservation and accepted by the US Department of the Interior in 2005.

The Schenck family farmhouse 2018. The right side was built in 1734, facing south, on a road that last appears on a 1945 land survey. The left side was built in 1816.

The rear of the house is what most people ever see. The cemetery is another 250 yards behind me.

Then I came across more house pictures from the 1940s, followed by some from around 1900, again featuring George Mann. A caption said that the Mann-owned farmland extended about a quarter mile west to what is now the site of the Village school, which meant it was formerly Schenck farmland. Nowhere did it say when the Schencks moved out and the Manns moved in.

By the end of February, I sent the group this email:

Bingo!

In about a week I will have a list of 25 graves, in three rows, courtesy of Ronald Burckley, former owner of the Schenck-Mann house. His father, Raymond, wrote them down. Ron also told me where other Schenck family members are buried. An important cemetery, as the crow flies, is about one block from the Mercy First family burial ground site. It's on the northwest side of today's Jericho Water Authority property. And there are other nearby historic cemeteries:

Syosset Cheshire Cemetery (102) between Miller Road, Edward Lane and Ira Road. Heavily vandalized by 1961. Inscriptions-Frost 1912; DAR 1941; TOB 1961. Schenck Cemetery (103) South of Jericho Turnpike at Jackson's Corner with 4 Schenck family burials 1877-1895. Inscriptions-DAR 1941. Schenck Family Cemetery (104) west of Our Lady of the Angels Home, approx. 300 ft north of Convent Road. Inscriptions-Frost 1912; DAR 1941; TOB June 23, 1962 plus additions Dec. 3, 1975. Unnamed Cemetery (105) corner of Miller Road and Colony Lane, north side of Miller, west of Colony. No stones or markers remained in 1961(TOB).

There's a lot to unpack here. I took the information Burckley provided at face value. He'd lived here all his life, and I assumed what he said was accurate. However, there were mistakes and omissions that came to light in 2024. I had contacted the national headquarters of the Daughters of the American Revolution (DAR) in Washington, DC, to see if they could tell me who had done the surveys listed above. DAR has visited literally every historic cemetery to mark the graves of those who fought in the Revolutionary War. In fact, it turns out that the DAR didn't visit the Schenck Burying Ground in 1941. That was done in 1932 by the Ketewamoke DAR Chapter of Huntington, Long Island.

I went to the other locations on Burckley's list but found only the Cheshire cemetery. It was a large mound next to a playground, with a four-foot fence around it. If it hadn't had a "Cemetery" sign, I wouldn't have known it was one. It had only three small stone tabs sticking out of the ground.

Just before Burckley delivered his father's list, Hammond emailed me two: The first was titled "Interments at the Schenck Cemetery East Woods (Syosset) L.I. Tombstone Inscriptions." (No name. No date.) It included 21 names in three rows. The second was a 1962 survey that Dean Velsor had documented for the Town.

I forwarded them both to the preservation group and started to track down "Inscriptions Frost 1912." Then Burckley stopped by.

I wrote the team:

Ronald Burckley just dropped off the same survey John found, as well as notes from his father written in 1945, and a 1984 letter from Ruth Davis, a descendant of Jan (John) Schenck who came to America from Holland in 1650. She said many of the Schencks were Baptized at the Old Dutch Reformed Church in Brookville (Wolver Hollow). The early records are in Dutch.

At the very end of the 1945 letter Burckley wrote, "Across the street in an early cemetery are buried about a hundred former residents of the Schenck house. Included are the inscriptions of three men who fought with George Washington during the American revolution."

Zach wrote back:

That's an astonishing number of gravesites, given the number of stones surviving. I suspect some of the Schencks were buried without markers, or with the nondescript fieldstones we've discovered, which have since disappeared.

I'm reviewing your emails, attachments and my own preliminary research. The Burckley notes will be invaluable and correspond to when the local DAR Chapter was recording burying grounds in the area (1941). Many of the stones recorded then are now illegible; others have disappeared entirely.

Probably the most important survey is Frost's (1912). From my experience, she recorded inscriptions in the order in which she found them, that is row by row and stone by stone. Later versions of her surveys often alphabetize her work, resulting in a loss of the relationships between the stones. It was important for us to secure a copy of the original survey referenced in Hammond's index for this reason.

I was in so far over my head that I asked Zach to please contact John Hammond directly about the Frost documents.

Hammond wrote back:

As I said in my Historic Cemeteries of Oyster Bay, Josephine Frost never personally recorded any cemetery inscriptions in the field herself. Her transcriptions are in the Queensborough Public Library and there is also a copy set in the New York Public Library; there may also be others. There is an on-line version in the Family History Library in Utah. However, these may not be helpful to you since it sounds like you are looking for the original field studies done by William Wyckoff from which Josephine Frost copied her transcriptions. Wyckoff was a member of the Long Island Historical Society and perhaps that is where you should look...

The original field studies, huh? William Wyckoff, huh? Suddenly this was daunting. I felt like a sprinter in a marathon. I told everybody I was headed for the New York Public Library on 42nd Street. If they didn't have the survey, nobody would. But Hammond said I would most likely have better luck with the Long Island Historical Society. Which, I would soon learn, had become the Brooklyn Historical Society in 1985. And while I was trying to contact them, I decided to check the internet. Lo and behold, I found a reference to the book and the volume, but not the Wyckoff notes.

Then I discovered there was a Wyckoff Museum in Brooklyn. So, after contacting Brooklyn Historical, I reached a James Scales, caretaker/beekeeper/operations manager at the Wycoff Farmhouse Museum on Clarendon Road, Brooklyn.

I wrote:

James, I have adopted the Schenck Family cemetery in Syosset through the Town of Oyster Bay. The cemetery has been vandalized and working with several historians we're trying to put it back together again. To do that, we need William Wyckoff's original field studies of LI cemeteries whose transcriptions Josephine Frost copied in 1912. From what I've learned, I believe the Schenck Family Cemetery is Volume 2, page 10. I can't find page 10. Where is page 10?

James replied:

To start: Do you know the title of the book you are looking for the 2nd volume of? We have a few editions of 'The Wyckoff Family in America' here. We may have other books in the attic, but I'm not sure if we have volumes of William Wyckoff's (William F. Wyckoff, of Jamaica, Queens?) field notes. Thanks.

Before I could respond, the very same day, Cecily Dyer, reference librarian, Brooklyn Historical Society, emailed me that she had found the notes. The pages were in my inbox. I couldn't believe it: Four pages in all, first recorded in 1902. The last page referred to a different location, "Two miles from Hicksville, Long Island, on the way to Syosset." There are four names on that page. I shared the email with all involved.

The search for the survey turned out to be a sprint after all. Everybody was excited.

Zach wrote:

Excellent! Please note that despite the preponderance of Schencks, they are not arranged alphabetically. We will need to compare these records with the surviving stone fragments, but because they appear to be recorded by rows in stone order, they should help us in identifying some that are illegible and others that are missing.

I was feeling pretty good about all this. But the fact remained that this was an obliterated graveyard. There was no way I could possibly make any sense out of all these surveys, or the ruins on the ground. I assumed the people I was working with could but had no idea how.

Plus, things still didn't jibe. Wyckoff/Frost had recorded 41 graves, with no mention of rows. Not everyone on the survey had the name Schenck. A few were named Marshall, two were named Lewis, one named Wanser, and the very last one was Baldwin.

The Burckley survey, which I, at the time, thought was the 1941 DAR document, recorded 21 names, in three rows, not 25, as Ron had said.

In 1962 Velsor recorded 20 graves, no rows. Some of his 20 names were different from the Burckley list. Velsor wrote at the beginning of his survey, "Two markers were lying face down and I was unable to lift them." I don't know whether he included them in his count. And at the end of the survey, he wrote, "There is one red sandstone marker in the cemetery. It is completely eroded and faceless.[7] 3 or 4 plain fieldstone markers." He also said the place was in poor condition. Which, I would soon discover, I incorrectly blamed on the Town. And nobody named Mann was on any list. It was time to remove the Mann name from the cemetery.

[7] The Burckley list says, "Brown stone, disfigured, age 35 years."

There was this other oddity, Garret Nostrand, who died on July 10, 1843. Nostrand's name was not on the 1912 Frost list of William Wyckoff's 1902 field notes, not on the 1940s Burckley list, and not on the 2007 Hammond list either. But somehow he's on the 1932 DAR survey and the 1962 Velsor survey. It didn't add up.

What went on here, and when, and who did it? And what happened to the 100 graves Raymond Burckley wrote about? Talk about a riddle wrapped in a mystery inside an enigma. We'll revisit Garret Nostrand later.

I wrote to Hammond, wondering where that 100 number had come from and asked if he thought the Frost survey was complete?

Hammond wrote back:

I would not put much trust in the anecdotal stories written in the past such as Tunison[8] in 1962-3; sometimes they have some excellent data but most of the time they just give an indication of where one needs to look for more information. As far as whether the list or any list for that matter is complete one never knows what is missing or what one does not have. Certainly, there are more graves than stones, it is still common practice not to place a stone or marker on every grave for various reasons.

I did not want to hear that. I found it hard to believe that Raymond Burckley, a schoolteacher, would just make it up. Nor would he invent that three of the people buried there fought in the American Revolutionary War.

I suppose I wanted the site to be historically more significant than it already was. And I suppose Burckley did, too. But I wasn't ready to give up looking for them and asked Zach if he ever used ground-penetrating radar in his work. The answer was yes, but he didn't think it was appropriate here, nor would it add much to the project, and it's quite expensive.

[8] Patricia Tunison wrote an article that was included in the Ron Burckley file that also said there were 100 graves.

CHAPTER 7

Phase 1: Palletizing the plunder

There was good news and bad news waiting in my inbox on March 13, 2019. The good news: It was the proposal from the Burying Ground Preservation Group. They were still on board. Kurt told me later on that they were actually having second thoughts from the get-go. This was quite an undertaking, and if things didn't go well, they had their reputations to consider. But Kurt said my "persistence, determination and willfulness," (translation: I was a pain in the ass) were enough to keep them from running and hiding, regardless of the outcome.

The bad news: Yours truly was the only good Samaritan paying for this.

SCHENCK-MANN BURYING GROUND, SYOSSET, NY

PHASE I WORK PROPOSAL:

Site assessment & probing, survey & recording, stone identification, cleaning & preparation for condition treatments & repairs

DAY 1

Photograph site as-is

Prepare pallets for organizing & cleaning stone fragments

Stake & number rows; label stones & fragments

Probe site for additional fragments; excavate & organize as appropriate

Begin pallet placement, stone placement

DAY 2

Complete pallet & stone placements

Photograph stones on pallets

Begin cleaning: wash w/ water & detergent, D/2 application

DAY 3

Complete cleaning: wash w/ water & detergent, D/2 application

Jigsaw fit stones and fragments

Photograph assembled stones and/or fragments

Estimated fees & expenses:

Fees: 2½ to 3 days @ $525/day x 2	***$2,625 - $3,150***
Supplies: D/2, orange mesh, misc.	***$400***
TOTAL PHASE 1	***$3,025. - $3,550***

It sounded reasonable enough. They didn't want a deposit but needed help scrounging at least a dozen more wooden pallets. I knew where there was a stack, and the owner said I could help myself. I passed the proposal along to the Town historian to see if the Town would pay for any of this or if I was on my own. Although I knew the answer in advance, I was still perturbed that the place had been totaled while it was under Town care, and I let Hammond know about it. He didn't take kindly to my hurling around accusations.

Meanwhile, Mark Kurnicki offered help cutting down a maple tree that was in the middle of many shattered gravestones. Some were literally engulfed by the tree. He said his guys would do it, once I showed him which one. I sent him a picture and almost immediately got a reply. "Done."

Mark's guys used a bucket truck and didn't add to the damage on the ground. I told him that after the historians gathered up all the fragments and cataloged and cleaned them, I would work on removing the stump. That was the only way to reclaim the marble fastened to the roots.

By the beginning of April, John Hammond was heading to the site to see what I had been up to. The weather was warming, and Zach was looking at his calendar to schedule me in for his Phase 1 work. We were kicking around the second week in April. Meanwhile, some workers had placed a 30-yard dumpster on Church property and the Church management thought I was the culprit. Angry emails started to fly. When Mark found out it was one of the Church's own vendors, he quickly apologized, emailing his bosses, the restoration team, and the Town. All good.

I dropped off a baker's dozen worth of pallets by a huge maple that stood at the entrance to the burying ground. The project was gaining traction. Given the number of broken stones, Zach wondered if we could get help from the kids who attended the school on the grounds. That was problematic, because the work would have to be

Getting the pieces out of the ground was the easy part.

A tangled mess. Some of the marble was literally attached to the roots.

done on a weekend. So Monday the 15th, 8:30 a.m. was penciled in for the work to start. The weather didn't cooperate, and we decided to move it back a day.

I wrote Mark that we would need a hose hookup for washing and cleaning the stones. He told me where it was and gave me a key for entering through a gate by the fenced-off area behind the Thomas Casey building and a key to enter the building itself, in case we needed to use the facilities.

Early in the morning of the 16th, I carried 200 feet of garden hose to the property and unlocked the gate to get to the faucet, and suddenly security guards surrounded me. I explained what I was doing, and they contacted Mark, who verified what I'd said.

When Zach and Kurt arrived, they started running cord to demarcate the rows. Based on where the stones were lying, they figured there were five rows. Once the lines were in place, somehow there was order to the chaos. By 11:00 a.m., Barney Levantino and his associate Jessikah Chautin from the library showed up for a look-see. Barney had a camera and a microphone and was taking pictures and recording the event for a podcast. Zach and Kurt took them on a tour.

After the librarians had left, the two restorers placed pallets all around the site; started photographing; and began putting fragments on the pallets, 18 in all. They used the term *palletizing* to describe the technique they had devised. When they removed a marble element, they placed a tongue-depressor-size stick in the spot where it came from. They numbered each stick and wrote the corresponding number on the pallet that became its temporary home. Some pieces started to fit together like a jigsaw puzzle. As Zach continued the process, Kurt would carefully take pieces to two other pallets. One for washing and cleaning, the other for drying. Once they were dried, he put them back where he found them.

The best use of my time became freeing up marble chunks entwined in tree roots. I used a bow saw and an ax to tackle what I could, while carefully avoiding the stones. Once in a while, I would find two touching pieces of marble buried one in front of the other, held in place by large tree roots. Somebody had buried them like that. Somebody had tried to preserve them. Somebody had worked here a long time ago—long enough for a tree to grow and lock the marble pieces in place. I wondered who?

Maybe it was the Sisters of Mercy. Maybe the place had been looted, vandalized, and restored several times. After all, the number of markers kept shrinking over the years.

At the end of the first day, I disconnected the hose and Zach and Kurt blocked off the entire site with orange mesh to discourage the curious. The following morning, they were back at it by 8 and continued the process while I went to the city for a doctor's appointment. When I returned, they were wrapping up for the day. Their plan was to finish the following Wednesday.

I gave back Mark's keys and concentrated on removing roots. Then I started on the tree stump left by Mark's crew. Barney, who returned to the site to take more pictures, suggested I use a portable Sawzall. A chainsaw blade would get dull the second it hit the ground. If I couldn't remove the stump, he said, he would come by and give me a hand. The easy job was freeing the touching tablets.

The large tree stump was something else. For that I also needed a shovel, spade, gardener's trowel, my ax, loppers, and a pry bar as well as three long and three short pruning blades for the Sawzall. I had never seen so many roots. Some were 8 inches thick. They crisscrossed and penetrated deep underground. They all needed to be cut to free the stump and then the marble. Before I could finish, the team returned to gather and clean the remaining fragments. When they left, I was back on my hands and knees working on the stump.

It wasn't until May 10 when, like an iceberg, the small piece of marble that was barely an inch above ground revealed itself to be a monster hidden beneath the surface. I freed it with chisels, placed it with a few other fragments on the nearest pallet, and notified the team. The reaction? "Incredible!" "Wow." "Congratulations." "Some job!"

Zach emailed:

Great job battling the stump! It's amazing how Mother Nature takes control. I guess all we can ever do is slow the process, although our group effort here has reversed many years of neglect. Kurt & I will return soon to spray the D/2[9] and batten down the hatches. Hoping Joel can swing by soon to provide cost estimates for the repair phase.

I was troubled by Zach's comment. We weren't doing this to slow down Mother Nature.

I dashed off an email, and included the Town historian:

I am concerned about the remaining trees with dead branches that will no doubt fall on the cemetery. The trees are too big to remove. The

[9] D/2 is a nontoxic antimicrobial solution used to turn dark, lichen-covered marble white again.

Zach, Jessikah Chautin and Barney Levantino of the Syosset Library, and Kurt being interviewed.

Someone had buried one piece of this desecrated tablet in front of the other to preserve them. But who? Counting rings established that the small tree was 40 years old.

Town never should have let them grow on this site. Perhaps next winter I can get a bucket lift and do some pruning. But first things first, getting an estimate from Joel on putting the stones back together and placing them where they belong.

Still no word from John Hammond and I'm getting worried. He's the only contact I have with the Town. Given the scope of the vandalism and the need for the Town's financial assistance with putting this back together, I'd appreciate any thoughts you might have on what to do?

Zach essentially said the Town's job was to mow and clean up limbs and debris. Not to restore the site. And not to do preventive maintenance. But it was difficult to accept this. Finally I got an email from Hammond. His system was down, and he was away.

I replied, copying the team and Mark Kurnicki:

Well, that's a relief. Glad you're in the pink, John. I've been on the road all day, busy last night and wanted to respond to Zach.

Zach, I appreciate your thoughts on the responsibility of the Town. However, I respectfully disagree and invite everybody to weigh in. Of the 126 or so cemeteries in Oyster Bay Town, of which half have been abandoned, the Schenck Family Burial Ground is not one of them. It is owned by the Town. Entrusted to it by the Schenck family, when it was horribly desecrated. The Town must have some kind of insurance, or the ability to raise funds to restore it. And, not just for the people of Syosset, but for the country. These are historic monuments to American History that the Town walked away from!

Furthermore, allowing trees, bushes and weeds to grow in the cemetery not only worsened the damage caused by the vandals, it created new damage and will cause even more down the road. The Town is culpable in damaging what they agreed to care for, and in my opinion, they should help pay for the repairs.

I'll be meeting Barney on Thursday PM at the Syosset Library for a podcast, perhaps this is an appropriate thing to talk about?

Hammond shot back a reply:

Could you please send me a copy or cite for me the source of 'it is owned by the Town, entrusted to it by the Schenck family.'

Ronald Reagan said one thing that I agree with and would learn the hard way: "Trust, but verify."

I wrote to Hammond:

While I've never seen anything in writing, my understanding is that in 1893 when the Schecnk family sold the property, in exchange for the road named Convent, the Town of Oyster Bay would care for the cemetery. If that isn't the case, then how is it that the parks department is mowing on Catholic Church property?

He didn't reply, nor did he have to. I felt so foolish and obviously didn't know what the heck I was talking about. Shame on me. Moreover, my accusations regarding the town's neglect damaged our relationship. I have the uncanny ability to put myself on people's shit list. It would be a long time before I heard from him again. And when I did, he was cold and distant.

My next failing was the podcast. Barney said it was great. It wasn't. Something went wrong with the recording, and I would have to do it again in August. When the day arrived, I was hot, tired, and distracted and left my reading glasses at home. I couldn't read my notes and winged it. It showed. Barney said I was fine. Believe me, I was pathetic, constantly grasping for words. I stammered and stuttered and said, "and uh" every few words. So much for preserving history. The only saving grace: Anybody listening would hit the delete button right away.

But the show must go on. So, I bought some topsoil to fill the hole left by the extracted tree stump. Mark joined me and said the next time I needed soil, I should ask him. And perhaps, so I didn't feel too bad, he added that he'd asked the Town many times to remove damaged and fallen trees and had gotten no reply.

Before the month was out, Kurt wrote that Phase 1 would be complete once Joel had examined the palletized stones to figure out what could be restored and how much it would cost. Then Zach would spray everything with D/2 and cover each pallet with orange mesh until Joel arrived to do the repairs. They would help him.

I wrote back to my cemetery angels, telling them that something had to be done about the trees. At least two needed to come down, and the bucket truck couldn't reach high enough. Mark figured that it would cost $2,000 a tree, if anybody would even do it. Kurt suggested that maybe I could find a tree guy who would donate his services. I didn't rule it out.

I needed to cut through at least 100 roots to free up the marble. Note the undamaged footstone in front of the stump.

It would take chisels to remove the marble from the tree. The still undamaged footstone in the background has the initials MES.

Two more pieces for the puzzle and no idea where they belong.

CHAPTER 8

Phase 2: Enter the trauma surgeon

Joel visited the site on May 30 to find out what he had to do. Zach and Kurt still needed to apply another coat of D/2, but the weather wouldn't cooperate. They needed three days in a row with no rain, or the solution would wash off. June 19 was the new target date. Meanwhile, I was still clueless about what Joel's work would cost.

Finally, at the beginning of August, I got an email from Zach:

Working from our inventory of 40+ headstones and footstones, we've identified 15 individual stones or groups of two or more matching pieces that are eligible for reassembling, reattaching and resetting in the ground.

An additional group of fragments may also be worth reassembling, but will not produce the same visual result.

Our recommendation is that we concentrate on restoring the first group of 15 stones (four are in the front row): seven are single stones that we'll reset; eight are groups of two or more matching pieces that require structural adhesives, clamping and cosmetic joint fills, and aluminum track braces to support them vertically in the ground. The work will take two full days for the three of us: Kurt, Joel & me. The work would be recorded photographically.

The projected cost is $5,000 inclusive of labor, supplies, travel, & insurance.

If this seems like a reasonable approach, we can provide you with a more detailed proposal. We can also look at the other group of stones when we're in the field, and talk about whether or not it's worthwhile to restore them as well.

There was an attachment from the Burying Ground Preservation Group, dated August 9, 2019.

SCHENCK-MANN BURYING GROUND, SYOSSET, NY

PHASE II WORK PROPOSAL:

Conservation treatment, 13-15 candidate stone monuments;

Repairs/restoration to include:

Reset to plum/level (7) large individual fragments

Reassemble, reattach multiple pieces (6-8) and reset

Photograph final site conditions

DAY 1

Preliminary cleaning to preform work as specified
Reset at grade/plumb level: 4 large candidate monuments (single fragments)
Reassemble, reattach (pin/adhesive): 4-5 candidate monuments (multiple pieces)

DAY 2

Reset at grade/plumb level: 3 large candidate monuments (single fragments)

Reassemble, reattach (pin/adhesive): 2-3 candidate monuments (multiple pieces

Reset at grade assemble monument pieces (6-8), utilizing non-corrosive "C" channel braces

Inset aesthetic fills at voids, cracks and holes as required

Final cleaning

Final photography

FEES & EXPENSES:

Fees: 2 days	***$5000***
Supplies, travel (included)	***$0***
TOTAL PHASE II	***$5000***

As the old saying goes: In for a dime, in for a dollar. I wrote back that it was acceptable and asked when they wanted to do the work. Zach said September or October, due to the summer heat. He hoped Barney would record it and asked me to contact Hammond, other Town officials, and the Historical Society to observe the restoration.

Barney said he had his hands full. His 96-year-old mom was in and out of the hospital, so his presence was doubtful. Hammond's curt reply was that the only obligation the Town had to the site was that New York state law required the nearest municipality to clear brush from abandoned cemeteries twice a year, and he had no interest in any podcasts. I knew no one else in the Town to contact and neglected to call the Historical Society, figuring they would follow Hammond's lead.

Zach was disheartened to learn that Hammond had essentially washed his hands of this and wrote:

> *It's disappointing to hear John's response to your efforts. What's the point of having a stewardship program? I'm Region II (Suffolk & Nassau) Coordinator for APHNYS (Assoc. of Public Historians of NYS) and I'm planning to launch a statewide effort to record and preserve historic cemeteries. Guess my thoughts will fall on some deaf ears!*

Either October 7–9 or October 21–23 were the dates the team had available. Unfortunately, the weather forecast for early October was against us, so we all penciled in the end of October. And separately, Zach agreed to do a presentation for the Syosset library the following January. He sent Barney a synopsis of his talk:

SAVING OYSTER BAY'S HISTORIC CEMETERIES

From the ancestral Underhill Burying Ground in Lattingtown to the long-abandoned Schenck Family Cemetery in Syosset, Oyster Bay Town contains many sacred and historic burying grounds. Despite periodic efforts to record and preserve them, however, monuments decay and inscriptions disappear.

Zachary N. Studenroth and Kurt E. Kahofer of the Burying Ground Preservation Group, Inc. will share their experiences resurrecting the Schenck Family Cemetery. Come and learn how you could help and share their passion for saving these vulnerable historic sites.

Joel and his son Koli drove up at 8 a.m. on the 21st in a white pickup towing a large trailer. Zach and Kurt arrived 30 minutes later. I stayed out of everyone's way and mowed the perimeter of the yard. A few hours after the critical care surgeons had begun, Ron Burckley arrived with his son. I introduced them to everybody and showed them the marble-covered pallets.

The work preceded at a snail's pace. Joel was precise with his level and carefully straightened and tamped bases firmly in the ground. Next he and Koli fit each piece to be drilled in place, making sure everything was snug. Koli held them together while his dad placed blue painter's tape in various locations on the lined-up sections of marble and marked drilling points on the tape. Then Joel turned over the top piece and clamped it securely to the stone tab it would be reattached to. He plugged his drill into a portable generator, donned a sophisticated face mask and goggles, and slowly and carefully started drilling holes in the bottom of the stones while Koli, also masked up with eyes protected, used an air gun connected to a compressor to blow the marble dust away.

As the Snodgrass team did their "triage," as Joel called it, Zach and Kurt were at another spot digging holes and standing up portions of headstones. Once they got everything plumb, they started to brush and clean the marble, which included applying a treatment of acetone on the areas that would receive adhesive.

The Burckleys never saw one fully repaired headstone before they left. I felt bad for them. Despite my zeal to show off what we had done, there was nothing to show. And even though all the marble had been cleaned and treated with D/2 months before, placing orange mesh material over the pallets to secure everything meant that the parts of the stone exposed to the sunlight had turned white whereas the parts touching the mesh were dark. So all the marble had a bizarre checkerboard appearance. It was hard to read the inscriptions.

Before the day came to an end and while Joel was working with Zach and Kurt mixing up epoxy and pinning, gluing, and clamping pieces together, Koli was widening the hole for Nelson Schenck's memorial. Much to everyone's delight, he found the top of Nelson's headstone. And there was a bonus. He also discovered a large broken fieldstone.

Koli cleaned the Nelson piece and applied acetone, and then Joel glued and clamped it in place. The day ended with Nelson's repaired monument back in place. There was no sign of his footstone.

I had mixed emotions, standing at the cemetery after everyone left. For starters, I didn't know what to expect. I just figured it would be much further along. I also had my worries about the pattern caused by the orange mesh. Nobody said much about it. I wondered if it would disappear or if we had compounded the problem. And then there were the trees. I could see rotten branches above me that could easily snap off and undo all the repair work going on. For all I knew, the trees had already done their share of damage.

The day after the repairs started, Zach sent me this:

After one day on site and with further discoveries, we have a better picture of which stones are eligible for conservation treatment. As originally projected, we

Joel Snodgrass and his son Koli drilling holes in the headstone of Nelson Schenck.

Koli found the top of the Nelson Schenck memorial. Nelson died July 23, 1852, age 19 years, 2 months, and 7 days.

were able to reassemble the fragments of fourteen individual stones which can be reattached and reset.

Eight of the fourteen require C-tracks to stabilize and support them, whereas the remaining six, after reassembly, can support themselves in the ground. Four stones were reset yesterday:

#10 Nelson Schenck: Assembled, pinned & reattached multiple pieces; reset

#26 Garret Nostrand: Reset

#30 Mary Schenck: Reset lower section; ready for reattachment of top

#33 Aaron Schenck: Reset lower section; ready for reattachment of top

We anticipate reattaching and/or pinning and resetting the following stones when we return:

#2 John Schenck: Reattach multiple pieces; reset with C-track

#3 Henry Schenck: Reattach multiple pieces; reset with C-track

#4 Jane E. Schenck: Reset (NB: also reset J E S footstone)

#7 Aaron Schenck: Reset with C-track

#19 Stephen Schenck: Reset with C-track

#21 William Schenck: Reattach multiple pieces; reset with C-track

#22 Stephen Schenck: Reattach multiple pieces; reset with C-track

#24 Cornelia Schenck: Reattach multiple pieces; reset with C-track

#37 John Schenck: Reattach multiple pieces; reset with C-track

An additional stone that was discovered as a result of the cleaning process and not represented in the survey will also be treated:

#41 Sarah Schenck: Reset

The remaining fragments appear insufficient at this time for reassembling and resetting. Unless further discoveries are made, these fragments can be saved and stored in your barn.

The list was formidable. Fourteen in all. Still a far cry from the Wyckoff/Frost survey. Let alone the 100 that Raymond Burckley wrote about in the 1940s. And maybe that was the best we could do.

I replied to Zach copying the team as well as Mark Kurnicki and Hammond:

Thank you, Zach. I'm forwarding this to John Hammond, who I'd also would like to thank for letting me adopt the Schenck Family burial ground. Through the combined efforts of all, we've saved this site for posterity. I can only say that I'm overwhelmed seeing those four headstones that have long been given up for dead, standing upright again!

John, we're waiting for some materials that Joel needs, so the work is on hold until next week. (Day TBD. I'll let you know.) I do hope you will join us. In fact, I hope you'll photograph the burial ground for the Town fathers to see. Perhaps they will promote your adopt a cemetery program so that others, like myself, will step in to help preserve both the Town and America's history.

And last, but not least, I have cc'd Mark Kurnicki who not only directed me to you, but has removed some trees on the site and has been incredibly supportive of the work we're all doing.

I must admit that even though I had what I thought were all the surveys of the site, I'd never paid much attention to them. That was the province of people like Zach, not me. The surveys were too intimidating. I still saw myself as a worker. The guy who rakes leaves, discovers marble elements, mows the lawn, and digs up tree stumps. What would I know about surveys?

On November 4, 8 a.m., a bright, brisk Monday morning, we reunited. Joel had placed orange flags everywhere. They told him what he had to drill, pin, and glue and where the repaired stones would go. The place was a beehive of activity. Zach doing painstaking cosmetic work between the cracks in the repairs. Kurt standing and straightening broken headstones and securing them in place. Joel and Koli drilling, digging, carrying, and setting their repairs.

Joel, the stone conservator, once again explained that given the mass of the mess, the best they could do was triage. He saw his role as stopping the bleeding.

I kept myself busy helping Kurt dig holes and straightening stones—and making occasional runs for coffee and sandwiches for the crew. When they needed my help to lift something, I was Johnny on the spot.

Marble is a soft stone, but it's stone nevertheless and heavy. The fact that so many large pieces were hurled all over the place and literally pulled out of the ground reminded us all of the ferocity of the vandalism. We kept theorizing about what happened. And it definitely had happened more than once.

Maybe it was wilding teenagers on a Friday night—hormones raging while they had nothing to do. Maybe it was a Halloween trick or a college fraternity haze. Maybe the stones that disappeared between 1902 and 1932 were taken for building materials. There was the Great Depression. Maybe it was a crazed loner who was desperate to show he was somebody by beating up on those monuments. In June 2022, a man was caught on camera at 2 a.m. on a rampage in the Historic Dutch Reformed Cemetery in Flatlands, Brooklyn, where other Schenck family members are buried. More than 300 years of history was destroyed in seconds. He was filmed kicking at headstones and lifting one up and carrying it away to smash on a walkway. And maybe somebody just drove over the site, as Kurt said. Or maybe it was all of the above.

It looked to me like Joel used almost every tool in his trailer that day. (Before his work was over, in 2023, he probably did.) He had his grandfather's spade and different kinds of shovels—one was the narrowest I had ever seen. He had drilling hammers, a vast assortment of gardening tools, 2 x 4s, pry bars, levels, metal clamps, wood clamps, straps, saws, shims, spacers, probes, glues, chemicals, and rags, and the generator that powered his drill bellowed most of the day.

To protect his work from being damaged by the clamps, he used pieces from heavy-duty black plastic bags. To protect the earth from piles of soil dug from around gravestones, he spread out other heavy-duty bags.

Somehow a completely eroded 40–50-pound tablet, which was moments from turning into a pile of marble muck, was gently dug up by the team. The four men then lifted it a few inches off the ground and slid it onto a large 5/8-inch plywood board that Joel produced from his bag of tricks. They would ultimately shroud it in more heavy black plastic bags and place it back where they found it, one grave over from Nelson's. Only propped up on a slight angle, so rainwater would run off. It remained like that, drying out, for more than two years.

Because it was right next to Nelson's grave, I went home and found the earliest survey (the brave soul that I am), and right next to Nelson's name, I found, "Jacobus Schenck, born May 26, 1791, died Jan. 17, 1873." Then I looked at the Burckley survey, and again, one grave from Nelson's, it said, "Jacobus Schenck (*stone reads Chenck*), died 1/17/1873, age 81 years, seven months and 22 days." Much to my chagrin, the two surveys rarely overlapped again, which disturbed me to no end. I didn't know which survey we were restoring to. The earliest, of course, being the most accurate. But too many headstones were missing. What to do? Easy. I put the surveys away.

Given the amount of work that remained and more discoveries, Kurt, Zach, and I were kicking around the need for a Phase 3. However, by the end of the day, thanks to everybody's efforts, the Schenck Family Burying Ground had five rows and was—excuse the expression—brought back to life.

I told Mark Kurnicki to expect Joel to stop by to make a few more repairs and collect his clamps. I was heading off on an eight-day two-man hike in Tuck-Up Canyon, Grand Canyon National Park. This would be an extreme hike in the remote western part of the canyon and give me a chance to see the Shaman Gallery. Discovered in the 1990s, it's a 60-foot-long, 900- to 3,000-year-old petroglyph.[10] I would also see the last active volcano in the Grand Canyon, Vulcan's Throne. It erupted a mere 73,000 years ago and dammed up the Colorado River.

Before I departed, I wrote John Hammond, sharing photos and apologizing, once again, for offending him. He never replied. The Burying Ground Preservation Group was copied.

Joel weighed in:

It really does look good, doesn't it? A far cry from the piles of loose/random stone fragments we looked at many months ago. It was encouraging that even more matches are being made as the process continues.

And you do deserve a lot of credit for making this happen; kind of amazing that not everyone sees it that way. History is something we all share. Have a great trip.

Zach also replied. He said that he and Kurt would return and set two more headstones while I was away—neither had an inscription but would serve as markers for grave sites. They would also inventory what was left to see if a Phase 3 was in the cards.

In my absence, they did return and Joel used noncorrosive exterior-grade structural supports called C-channels to stand the top portion of yet another Aaron Schenck. Still missing was the rest of his marker. Zach and Kurt applied D/2

[10] The remarkable artwork has already been defaced. Someone graffitied the name Michael across it.

to everything. But Zach wasn't happy. Something wasn't right with the C-channels. They were covering some of the letters on the inscriptions and needed to be cut.

On that score, Joel wrote:

> *Yes/agreed regarding the braced stones. To clarify - the stones are in the "dry-fit" stage, meaning they have an initial test set in the braces, and they are up off the ground to allow drying out, but we need to come back, remove the stones from braces and cut, trim, shore the braces as necessary to be aesthetically finished and refit the stones properly. That was the original plan and would have been done that same day while we were there but the cutting blades were expended and daylight was ending, which makes work unsafe/problematic, so a follow-up day was planned. We also encountered a problem with the last stone setting becoming loose when it was picked up by the three of us, so that needs to be checked as well and possibly reset again. Koli has been away so we're working out a return date to get this taken care of as part of the work.*

This is one of the largest markers at the site. It belongs to John Schenck, first son of the John Schenck who died June 27, 1804.

Kurt and Zach found most of John's tablet. Here they're getting it ready for gluing. Joel has the clamps, straps, and shims.

The troublesome mesh pattern would ultimately disappear.

Koli and his dad standing up John Schenck's marker. That stone would be moved two more times before this project was over.

Zach applying white mortar on one of the Aaron Schencks.

Kurt Kahofer is setting a partially repaired nameless headstone, which would be moved again. The pedestal base to his left has a small inscription on one end: Sutter Hicksville.

We know who made at least one of the headstones.

Daniel Sutter

Daniel Sutter died Saturday morning, July 8, in his 90th year, at his home, 23 Newbridge road, Hicksville. He was the father of seven sons and one daughter. Four sons and one daughter survive him: Fred, Richard, William, Frank and Mathilda Sutter, also eleven grandchildren and seven great-grandchildren. Mr. Sutter has lived in Hicksville 37 years and was a senior member of the firm of Daniel and Fred Sutter, monumental business. He was a member of Herder Lodge No. 698, F. & A. M., over sixty years. Masonic services were held at his home Tuesday, July 11, at 8 o'clock.

Funeral services were held at his home Wednesday, July 12, at 2 P. M. Burial was in Plainlawn Cemetery, Hicksville.

that's our formula for securing the Monumental business of the particular public. We solicit but a chance to show you the character, workmanship and quality of our stones—and to quote prices—for we know then that you will place your order with us.

Will you give us that chance?

Call and see our assortment of several hundred finished Monuments, Headstones, Etc.

D. & F. SUTTER
Hicksville, L. I.

Tel. 76-M. Oppo. Railroad Depot.
Granite Survey Posts Always on Hand.

DANIEL SUTTER FRED SUTTER

SUTTER MONUMENTAL WORKS

Telephone 76 **HICKSVILLE, L. I.** Opp. L. I. R. R. Depot

WORK ERECTED IN ANY CEMETERY

CALL AND SEE AN ASSORTMENT OF SEVERAL HUNDRED FINISHED MONUMENTS, HEADSTONES, ETC.

GRANITE SURVEY POSTS ALWAYS ON HAND

Kurt found Daniel Sutter's obituary: 1843–1933. Unfortunately, no records remain from the Sutter Monumental Works.

November 4, 2019: the end of Day 2, Phase 2.

Five rows of graves and the yet-to-be-determined.

Brought back from oblivion, the headstone of yet another John who died in 1838, age 29.

CHAPTER 9

A bureaucratic snafu

Snow was on the ground when December rolled around. There wasn't much I could do.

My friend in Bremerton, Washington, Bill Hoke, a copywriter, editor, and mountaineer extraordinaire, was fascinated by the restoration project and kept sending me articles on LIDAR and ground-penetrating radar. As much to humor him as knowing there were so many missing pieces hiding underground, I pestered Zach about the technology.

Zach responded to my email:

... "It's not like prospecting for remains; it's a slow, steady process of reading evidence of sub-soil disturbances which are shovel marks left from digging burials. It can locate gravesites but can't tell you anything about the person. And it's expensive, but without training, the average person wouldn't know how to read the images."

I wouldn't let go and contacted a company called Subsurface Solutions. They assured me that their equipment would locate the missing stones, but they don't rent it out. However, they gave me the contact information of one of their customers who might be able to help. The man asked me a battery of questions ranging from the soil type to surface conditions to the size of the cemetery.

He said the system costs $35,000 and I had to insure it, transport it, and put up a lot of money for a deposit, and I was on my own on how to use it. He ended his communication by suggesting that since it's such a small area, I should just dig it up by hand to find the missing stones. "It's a good workout."

I laughed and told Hoke that's what I would do.

After the snow cleared, Joel still had the glued-together, battered remains of Henry Schenck's headstone bound and strapped to the aluminum braces. He wanted to come over and pick up his gear. We met at the site midmonth, and I told him I wanted to clear the jungle of honeysuckle, greenbrier, and downed tree limbs in the northwest corner of the graveyard, figuring it was so close to the burial mound that I wouldn't be surprised if headstones were hidden there. He thought it was a good idea.

He also pointed out a row of small maples along the north fence that I should get rid of before they turned into full-grown trees. I agreed and told him that when I finished clearing, I'd start searching for fragments. I asked him to please order a probe for me so I could explore the underground.

Clearing the overgrowth took three days. My machete, lawn mower, loppers, a weed whacker, and chainsaw for the fallen tree limbs all came into play. Frustrated by the trees growing behind me, I contacted Mike's Trees.

Mike was a cop who had a side business as a tree and stump remover and had done some work for me in the past. He came to the cemetery, and I showed him the two 70-foot cherry trees that were my immediate concern. He said he wouldn't go near them. He got the creeps just being there.

I contacted another tree guy, Bill at Brandywine Tree Service. The power company had given me his name, because I needed some limbs cut that were hanging over the wires on my property (something else Mike's Trees wouldn't touch).

Bill was in Florida by his dying father's bedside. I told him what I needed and mentioned the trees at the cemetery. He said he would have a look when he got back in town. However, I would need permits before he would remove any trees on Town-owned land. Which meant it was time to talk to John Hammond, the Town historian, about tree permits.

He didn't reply. I emailed him, and he finally wrote back that I had the contact information for the Parks Department, saying they issue permits if any are necessary. I replied, "I have no contacts there. You're the only one I know in the Town." Hammond replied, "Joseph Pinto is the Parks Commissioner." He included his phone number.

When I called Commissioner Pinto, he said he had no idea anybody had adopted a cemetery in the entire Town and that he was the only one who could allow me to adopt the site. Furthermore, he was opposed to removing healthy trees even from a historic cemetery. Uh-oh.

I explained that Hammond had granted me permission. I'd signed some kind of contract and had been working there for about a year. He asked me to email him all my communications with the Town historian.

Zach and Joel were both disheartened by the news. Zach said that if I needed a letter from professional restoration consultants to help get things back on track, he would write one.

Commissioner Pinto received my email, which I copied Hammond on, and he replied that during the past year, the Town had initiated an Adopt-A-Spot program and gave me the phone number for his associate, Christopher Sabellico, who would guide me through the process of officially adopting this location. Unfortunately, the commissioner couldn't shed any light on how long the Town had been caring for the cemetery.

Then Hammond sent an email to the commissioner and copied five Town officials and me. He attached Town resolutions on the Abandoned Cemetery Adoption Program and the indemnification document I'd signed. Surprisingly, Hammond stated, "There is no contract between the Town and any party involved in the cemetery adoption program."

I immediately wrote the commissioner, copying everyone the historian had copied, and thanked him for his reply. I told him I'd assumed what Hammond had me sign was a contract and that that was all he'd asked for. I took full responsibility for whatever had happened and stated that my interest was in saving the cemetery. No costs had been incurred by the Town. Everything was out of my pocket, and I would be happy to work with Mr. Sabellico so I might continue. But I still needed guidance on the trees. They needed to be removed to prevent further ruin. If anyone wanted to walk the property with me, I believed they would agree that the trees do not belong on top of a grave.

Chris Sabellico was my next email. Once again, I cc'd everybody and laid out for Chris what was going on, telling him that two phases of the restoration were completed, whom I was working with, and what needed to be done. I also sent photos of several pallets filled with fragments and restored headstones in the background—including the maple tree with all the shattered marble around it—and added that I wouldn't do any more work until I'd heard from him.

Chris was a sweetheart of a guy. He wrote back:

...It sounds like you are dedicated to your restoration project, and that is appreciated. I observed the photos, and I think I understand the plan of the project and where you are going from here. I would love to meet you at the

site at your earliest convenience to see it first hand and meet you, and we could look at the two trees of which you speak.

He included an Adopt-A-Spot application. We arranged to meet Wednesday, December 18, 2019. In the meantime, I filled out the adoption form. Zach looked it over, and then I snail-mailed it back to Chris.

Although I didn't do any more work, I did do something else. I started matching the pieces on the pallets. That worked two ways: First just standing and staring at the fragments and then putting the possible matches on an empty pallet where I would move the elements around to see if they fit. Keep in mind that, unlike with a jigsaw puzzle, I didn't always know if the stone was right side up or not. Especially if it had no writing. There was a lot of trial and error.

And second, since I had photographs of all the pieces, I laid them side by side on my computer screen and looked for matches that way. If I saw something promising, I returned to the cemetery to see if they fit together. Sometimes the typography was the giveaway. Sometimes it was the color or texture of the marble. Sometimes the width. And sometimes the computer, which automatically changes pictures on my desktop every minute, would zoom in on an element and trigger something in my subconscious.

As the process advanced, I walked the site, tape measure in hand, to try to find homes for the palletized fragments. If I saw something interesting, I'd carry over the potential match.

A case in point was William Schenck, who passed away November 20, 1844. He lived 51 years, 5 months, and 16 days. The top of his gravestone had been reassembled during Phase 2 and was supported by C-channels. I carried four fragments of scripture I had pieced together to the headstone to see if they belonged.

Looking around me, I noticed the footstone with the initials MES still in the ground, where it always had been. A lightbulb went off. That footstone reminded me that I'd dug up a huge tree stump nearby—and with it a substantial piece of marble. Could that be the base of William's headstone?

Off to the pallets I went to find the large stone. Then I laid it on the ground next to the scripture. Voilà, the pieces fit. Carefully lifting the heavy headstone from the support braces, I found that it also fit the scripture. I was so excited that I couldn't

Pieces of William's scripture reassembled.

Initially, this was all we thought existed of William Schenck's marker.

It would take two more years before William's headstone was back in the ground.

wait to tell everybody. I found so many matches this way, but it would take years before William's headstone was standing sentinel over his grave again.

On the morning of December 18, Chris Sabellico was waiting for me at the Schenck burial site. He was fascinated by what he saw and distressed by the carnage. I pointed out the problematic trees and couldn't have had a more sympathetic ear. He said it's hard to tell what was caused by tree damage and what was vandalized and that he would talk to the commissioner about the trees.

Showing him the William Schenck discovery, I told him I was eager to get back to work. The weather was cooperating, and he had no problem with our continuing the restoration while he navigated the adoption papers through the Town.

The next two finds were pieces of yet another Aaron Schenck and a hodgepodge of unidentifiable marble chunks that fit together. I had no idea where any of it belonged. There were so many missing pieces. But I was gaining confidence that there would be a Phase 3. I sent pictures of the discoveries to everyone.

Joel wrote back:

Great results. You are becoming a sleuth! Time and patience (and a knack at jigsaw puzzles) really helps! Lol. That's some amazing stuff.

"A sleuth!" I liked the sound of that.

Much to the annoyance of my wife, I was spending more time with the departed Schencks than with her. So, I shifted gears and grabbed the dogs and cats, and we went to Montauk for a few days. Although living in the old Syosset farmhouse is like living in Maine, only surrounded by all the amenities of suburban life, living in Montauk is like living in a National Park. In both cases, I'm happy. Happy to be away from people and connected to nature. Yet I was chomping at the bit to get back to work on my lifesize jigsaw puzzle.

We returned to Syosset a few days before Christmas. It was early Christmas Eve when Bill from Brandywine called. His dad had passed away and he was back in New York. He said he would stop by in the morning. I asked him if he would be coming down the chimney? He laughed.

Little did I know that Brandywine Tree Bill was William Goldberg—the only Jewish tree climber on Long Island. When he told me that, I said, "Well, I'll bet I'm the only Jew restoring a Protestant Cemetery on Catholic Church property on Long Island." We both laughed.

Bill and I met at the house and then walked over to the cemetery. He saw the trees and said, no problem. He wouldn't damage the gravestones, quoted me $800 a tree, told me he was licensed and insured, and reminded me that I needed permits before he would do any work. What a relief, I thought. Two trees for less than what Mark figured one would cost. I told him I'd get back to him.

By the 29th, I found more pieces of that marble hodgepodge. It turned out to be another Jane Schenck. She died March 15, 1846, age 62 years, 4 months.

Zach wrote:

Looks like we'll have to find a spot for her... I just looked up "Jane Schenck" in Hammond's Guide and found both of them at the site in 2007. Major damage must have occurred after he published the Guide.

I could only do so much staring at the pallets. It was time to start probing the ground. Although I didn't have an actual probe, I did have a pitchfork. Starting in the southwest corner, it was much easier to put four prongs in the dirt and carefully step down on the crossbar than to try to push a single probe into the ground by hand. The limitations? I could go down only 4 or 5 inches. The pitchfork often got stuck. More times than not, I'd hit a rock or got the pitchfork jammed in a root and had to jerk it free. I'd move it around and probe and probe and probe again. If I still found resistance, I'd grab my shovel and trowel and carefully dig.

Almost immediately I hit pay dirt around the "Sutter Hicksville" pedestal and sent everybody the picture. I thought the piece had "1818" written on it. Kurt said it was too dirty to tell but that he would cross-reference the date with older inventories to see if he could find out whom it belonged to. I left it where I found it.

It rained on New Year's Eve, but it was warm enough to keep working on New Year's Day. When I got to the cemetery, the rain had splattered everything with mud. What a mess. There was nothing I could do about it but wait another day and buy a portable spray container like the one Joel used. It held 2½ gallons of water, and Home Depot has them. Unfortunately, splash-back would be a recurring theme until the grass grew.

I grabbed the pitchfork and kept probing. Every foot or so, I'd step on it, pull it out of the ground, and do another foot. I kept a pile of rocks in a flowerpot and used them to mark the borders of where I had probed. To mark the perimeter, I used those 3-foot-long orange driveway markers that people use when it snows.

Like finding a needle in the haystack: This random little piece fit perfectly.

Buried inches from the "Sutter Hicksville" pedestal base, this looked like it said "1818" on first glance.

The pitchfork hit these marble fragments hidden under a tree.

Another surprise: a third Aaron Schenck!

Welcome back, Jane Schenck, February 15, 1784–March 15, 1846.

A miracle: The bottom left corner of the newly reassembled Jane fit perfectly on the tab by the tree.

Rebuilding Jane II was a project in itself. Finding out where she goes turned out to be incredibly gratifying.

Each time I covered another foot of ground, I'd move the stones and the orange markers. It was, as the man said, "a good workout."

On the morning of the 2nd, I purchased a large spray container, filled it with water, and carried it over to the site. It took a good hour, including a refill, to wash all the mud off the marble. Next I decided to search for the low-hanging fruit. That meant probing around the tabs that nobody had touched during the restoration.

The first place I tried was by the trunk of one of the 70-foot trees. The pitchfork hit something right away. I grabbed the shovel and trowel and found that, just behind the small headstone, were a few large fragments somebody had buried. Behind them, and deep underground—literally under the tree—was more of the same stone. The tape measure confirmed the widths and lengths. I dug up what I could and laid the pieces on the ground. The piece under the tree stayed put.

Along with pieces of the gravestone was a small broken-in-two footstone. It had the initials NAS. That could be only one person: Nelson Schenck.

Elated, I sent photos to Zach, Kurt, and Joel and also to Chris, expressing an even more urgent need to remove those trees. This really was someone's grave I was talking about.

Every now and then, I have a eureka moment. On January 10, eight days after my discovery, I was staring at the white tab by the tree. On impulse, looking off in the distance at the hodgepodge on the pallet that had become a second Jane Schenck, I walked over to it, picked up the bottom left-hand piece, and carried it over to the tab by the tree. It fit perfectly. I couldn't believe my eyes. I had found where Jane II was laid to rest.

Nobody will ever know how Howard Carter felt when he discovered King Tut's tomb, but I knew that this was as close as I would ever come.

Fast-forward to 2:00 p.m. on January 16, 2020. Barney Levantino had rolled out the red carpet for us at the Syosset library. It was time for the presentation by the Burying Ground Preservation Group on the Schenck restoration.

Still reeling from my dreadful podcast, I was happy to sit in the audience with 20 other people and keep my mouth shut. The experts, Zach and Kurt, spoke about the restoration. Joel was available to answer questions. When the program was over, Barney asked the four of us to sit down and do another podcast. At least I sounded lucid this time.

Half an hour later, the team and I left the library and went to the burying yard to examine their work. They saw what I'd reassembled in their absence and were impressed enough to commit to a Phase 3. Before heading to my house for what would become an annual wine tasting event and to toast our success, friendship, and the long-departed who'd brought us all together, the four of us carried the remaining pallets to the east side of the cemetery. With all the pieces in one place, we figured, it would be easier to find more matches.

CHAPTER 10:

This just in from the Town

After the guys left the wine tasting, I checked my emails and found a message from Chris Sabellico. He said the paperwork for the adoption was still in limbo. The lawyers weren't clear on who owned what. As to the trees, there was a new tree surgeon working for the Parks Department whom the commissioner wanted me to meet. Apparently, the photos I'd sent Chris had the desired effect. But there was more. The Town attorney gave him permission to release the following to me:

Along with a drawing of the boundaries of the site and extensive tax information on the tax-exempt Church, as well as the locations of various historic cemeteries in the area, there was a 1985 reply to a letter from a Ruth Davis in Whippleville, New York. Apparently, she'd requested all the available information on the Schenck cemetery. The reply, written by Oyster Bay Town Clerk Ann R. Ocker, included the 1962 Velsor survey, which was provided to her by D.H. McGee, the Town historian at the time. The letter said that considerable time had gone into compiling the information and that "…access to this cemetery, which is privately owned, will require permission from the owner."

If I understood this correctly, that meant that in 1985 the Schenck Family Burying Ground was still owned by the Catholic Church. Therefore, the looting and the desecration happened under their watch. And there was more. Typewritten on St. Mary of the Angels Home letterhead, dated August 30, 1957, and received by the Town clerk, September 3, was this:

The Town Board

Town Hall

Oyster Bay, L.I. N.Y.

Gentlemen:

Permit me to direct your attention to the existence of a number of graves on our property where people were interred apparently many years prior to our purchase of the land.

I wonder if either Sec. 291, providing for the care of graves, or Sec. 296, dealing with the relocation of remains in an abandoned cemetery would be applicable here.

I would appreciate your investigating this matter since the plot referred to is in deplorable condition.

Respectfully yours, Sister Mary Austin, Supt.

The letter was signed in longhand.

So, as far back as 1957, the cemetery was in "deplorable condition" and "abandoned." But who abandoned it? The Church had owned the land since 1893. It's obvious that the Schenck cemetery had been severely damaged time and again. Half the headstones disappeared between 1902 and the middle of the century. As to its being transferred to the Town back when the Church first bought the land, well, that was pure fiction. The slings and arrows I hurled at the Town had been misdirected. The truth is, the desecration did not happen while the Town owned the land. John Hammond, if you ever read this, once again I apologize.

James Henry's elements were my next discovery. Zach didn't recall seeing his name. That forced me to dig out the surveys, even though they were still anathema to me.

I found James Henry right away. He was first on the Frost survey and No. 10 of 11 in the first row on Burckley's. On the Velsor survey, he was 10 of 20. All of this was so confusing that I asked Zach, "How is it that he's in a different location on every survey?"

"Simple. Every surveyor approached the site from a different direction."

In 1902 William Wyckoff started in the northwest corner, recording from left to right. In the 1940s, Burckley started in the southwest corner, recording from right to left. And Velsor came at it from the east (which happens to be the oldest part of the cemetery). The Daughters of the American Revolution (1932) and Hammond (2007) listed the names alphabetically.

It occurred to me that since Burckley had him at No. 10 of 11 graves, and Frost No. 1, between 1902 and the 1940s, somebody replacing James Henry's headstone put it one spot away from where it was originally. Who was that somebody? Is it possible that some of the nuns had put a stop to the stripping of the cemetery and just put it back in the wrong place?

James Henry coming together: His headstone is located in a different place on each survey. The piece on the bottom left became known as the "New Hampshire" stone.

A large fieldstone marker whose broken halves were at least 50 feet apart.

Zach and Kurt found most of Martha's stone. SISE and the scripture piece came later.

The piece tucked into the right C-channel belonged to Henry Schenck's gravestone. The others have yet to find a home.

Brownstone pieces buried far away from where they belong.

There was no way to reattach them.

The next discovery was that the piece of marble I thought said "1818" didn't. It said "SISE." Martha Van Sise. It fit perfectly in her headstone. I also located her scripture. Still missing was the base.

When I showed the photo to the team, Zach sent back her genealogy. Martha Boerum Schenck, born June 18, 1837. Died April 29, 1864. She married Andrew Van Sise around 1855. They had two children, Charles and Emma.

Meanwhile, Chris from Parks said the lawyers were holding up the adoption, because they still didn't know the exact metes and bounds of the cemetery. They were working on it. Chris also had someone else in mind to cut the trees. He introduced me to Vinny Siviano, who met me on January 31. Vinny didn't have any equipment, though, and wouldn't for three more weeks. But my sense was that he would be able to take care of it.

Back when Koli discovered the top of Nelson Schenck's headstone, he had found a large broken fieldstone. That was on the west side of the site. I dug up the other half all the way over on the east side.

As I said, every minute, my computer randomly changes the photos on the desktop and zooms in on them, too. Through it, I found that we had missed the bottom right-hand corner of Henry Schenck's smashed headstone. It's one of the most damaged of them all.

Next the pitchfork hit a buried pedestal base behind a broken headstone. Along with it were a dozen brownstone fragments that were nowhere near the solitary decaying marker they came from.

Probing the earth was getting as monotonous as staring at the pallets. To break it up, I borrowed my friend's portable Sawzall and started cutting old tree stumps level to the ground. The fact that the remains of half a dozen trees were so obvious once again made me wonder who had cut them. And who had buried those brownstone fragments. And what was the reason they didn't bury them next to the brownstone headstone?

My wife owns a champion scent dog named Fiona. Every week in the winter, we'd head out to Montauk and Sandy worked the dog in the farm fields in East Hampton. On one trip back to Syosset, we heard Southampton Town Supervisor Jay Schneiderman being interviewed on the local public radio station. He said Southampton had just purchased a state-of-the-art 3D ground-penetrating-radar machine, to look for Colonial as well as Native American burial sites so developers couldn't build on that land.

The supervisor and I have known each other for more than 40 years. I sent him a text telling him I'd heard him on the radio and what I was doing in Oyster Bay and asked if I could borrow the machine, lent municipality to municipality. I would pay for his technician. He said, "Fine with me. But I would have to check with the Town clerk, Sundy Schermeyer, who is in charge of the equipment." Jay sent me her phone number. Once again, I couldn't believe my good fortune and called the clerk and spoke to her assistant.

The message I left for Ms. Schermeyer was that I was working with Zach, the former Southampton town historian, on a cemetery restoration and we could really use that machine. Unbeknownst to me, the relationship between the two was toxic. Zach filled me in, and when I spoke to the Town clerk, she told me her side. None of which mattered. The clerk informed me that they were still training on the machine and it would be tied up for years. Then came the zinger. When Southampton bought it, covenants and restrictions were put in place to make sure it would never leave the Town.

Schermeyer was very supportive, though, and put me in touch with the current Town historian, Julie Green, and a gentleman named Roger Tollefsen, who were both working to find lost grave sites in Southampton. They assured me that the technology was not right for my rock-filled, root-riddled subsurface.

Yet even without the radar, I was still finding more broken stones. In fact, there were so many new finds that Zach wrote:

> *We're all excited about your discoveries. Seems as if we should meet back at the site, whenever you feel it's time, to assess where we go from here. Keep exploring!*

And that's exactly what I did. I told Zach we should wait until early spring.

CHAPTER 11

Stayin' alive. Ah, ha, ha, ha, stayin' alive.

I knew that this wasn't the Taj Mahal we were restoring, but the high from saving a lost and forgotten window to the past inspired me to keep on going. And as fate would have it, something else would, too.

Sandy and I went to South Florida for an end-of-February vacation. Our plan was to stay a week, head back to New York, and then go to Florida again in March to watch the 2020 Miami Open Tennis Championship. Before we left Miami, we met a couple for dinner in South Beach. The man in the party kept pointing to his chest and complained he couldn't breathe. He had compromised health to begin with and needed help just to get to the table. Two days later he died. The hospital said it was from his preexisting condition. But given what was about to unfold, that might not be the whole story.

His body was flown back to New York, and Sandy and I attended the funeral the first week in March. What struck me during the service were all the mourners. The room was packed. Maybe 150 people attended. There was so much sadness.

For the first time, it really sank in that back in the nineteenth century, many Schenck family members stood at their little burying yard behind their house, with their eyes filled with tears, as they bid farewell to someone they loved. A mother, a father, a grandparent, a friend, a confidant, their brothers and sisters, aunts and uncles—the ones they laughed and cried with. And their children. Indeed, there are four tiny headstones, one right next to the other, all belonging to infants—all obliterated. The monuments that marked their lives were very important to the living, just like they are today. Visited on birthdays, holidays, and anniversaries. With flowers placed by the gravestones. It all made me feel sad.

We never returned to Miami. By March 14, the first official fatality from COVID-19 was announced in New York. Not long after that, we found ourselves in a worldwide pandemic. One of the symptoms: having trouble breathing. It would be years before I was ever in a crowd as large as the one in that funeral home.

Ultimately Sandy and I moved ourselves and the animals to Montauk to get as far away from bad air, and other people, as possible. But for the time being, we were completely safe, in total isolation. Sandy in the old farmhouse and me with my pitchfork in hand, probing the ground, searching for ruins, surrounded by the long departed.

As to the trees, well, we were all happy that the Town might take them down and save me from paying for it. Dream on, Rav. The coronavirus killed that, too. It was back to plan A: pay Brandywine $1,600 to remove the trees.

Back at the burying yard, I discovered a large section of Stephen Schenck's headstone and sent pictures to the team. It was so obvious that the guys laughed because they couldn't believe they'd missed it. Who can blame them? There were so many broken stones and so many repairs. Hey, this wasn't like looking at the picture on the box that a jigsaw puzzle comes in to see where things go.

Before the month was out, Joel wrote everybody that he wouldn't be returning to work anytime soon. He'd tested positive for COVID!

Nearly a month later, he was finally feeling better but had no energy. Lucky me: By then I was photographing migrating gannets over the Atlantic and taking solitary walks along the Montauk beach with the dogs. Then once a week, I left Montauk for Syosset to do my grocery shopping, water the plants, and spend a few hours searching and sleuthing.

By the end of April, everybody had cabin fever. Sandy was tired of cooking and spending so much time alone. Joel was fed up with being in quarantine. Kurt and Zach were anxious to get back to Syosset and continue the restoration. To keep themselves from going crazy, they started working on a new book about the old schoolhouses of Long Island. There's actually one right down the street from us in Montauk.

And Chris Sabellico, like every other Town employee on Long Island, was resigned to working in isolation from home during the lockdown. Cemetery 104 was no longer a priority. The best I could hope for was to keep it on the radar screen.

The month of May came and went. In the beginning of June, I extended my stay in Syosset so I could mow the cemetery. By the end of the month, Chris wrote me to say that the Parks Department would no longer be mowing the site. The job had been transferred to the Highway Department. When I heard that, I told him I

A perfect fit for Stephen Schenck. Born March 29, 1824. Died May 12, 1876.

Sarah, wife of James Ellison, slowly coming together.

wanted to be there when they arrived so they wouldn't damage any of the work in progress. He understood.

Then in mid-July, I got a request from him to fill out another Adopt-A-Spot application form and, although I was still not the official land steward, a hold-harmless waiver from the Town attorney's office, so I could eliminate those trees.

Not long after that, I met up with the Highway Department, and when they were finished mowing, the place looked better than I had ever seen it. One of the men doing the work was of Dutch ancestry. He bent over backwards to do this right—telling me his mother used to take him to visit the old family graves in Oyster Bay when he was a boy.

Chris told me there was one other change in the works: The Town had assigned Louis LaRusso, an employee of the Highway Department, to be in charge of maintenance for all the abandoned Oyster Bay cemeteries.

Louis and I met in August. He was anxious to help and couldn't have been nicer. However, his role was limited. After Labor Day, he returned to his day job as a schoolteacher. Louis sent me a map of the property. When I looked at it, it was abundantly clear that nobody knew exactly what the Town owned and what the Church thought the Town owned.

While in Montauk, thanks again to the computer, I was piecing more stones together. I'd find potential matches with the pictures—blowing images up, rotating them around, and placing them next to other photos. The colors, shapes, textures, and typography got ingrained in my mind. I'd make notes, and when I returned to Syosset, I'd see if the pieces fit. Sarah, wife of James Ellison, came together this way.

There is no way Zach, Kurt, or Joel could have done this. They would have had to live with the puzzle the way I did. Both at the site and virtually, day after day. Nobody else would do that. Nor could I afford to pay someone to.

Finally, late that summer, the Burying Ground Preservation Group was back at work. They were restoring the Parsons Cemetery in Springs, a hamlet of the Town of East Hampton. When they finished in Springs, their plan was to head to Syosset to meet me. They figured two days in October or early November was all they needed in order to finish the job. Perfect timing, because I had the Brandywine Tree Service booked for August.

However, it was October 2 when the crew finally arrived to remove the trees. Several tons of wood came down that day. No damage to the monuments. And, at last, I was approved as the official caretaker for the site.

What a relief it was to have this behind me! And clearly something I never expected when we started. The guys said that by eliminating the trees, we would add another 50 years to the life of the cemetery. Hopefully at that point, another anonymous someone will come along and give the place a helping hand. It certainly happened before.

Zach, Kurt, and Joel were still finishing up a job in Setauket. The weather held them back, and I didn't see them again until six days after the November election. Unfortunately, Kurt couldn't make it. He was caring for his mom.

Two days turned into three. Zach was digging up paired headstones buried in the northwest corner. Joel was busy straightening and prepping the base of Jane's headstone hidden under the now-defunct tree. Then he drilled into the stone and started the slow rebuilding process.

As the glue was fixing on Jane II, the team started to glue Martha Van Sise; followed by William; and after that, Henry. Then the most significant thing of all the things in three days of significance happened.

On a hunch, Zach carried the script portion of the Van Sise headstone to the southernmost tab that was flush to the ground in the western corner of the graveyard. It was a perfect fit. I was bowled over.

And because he did that and because Jane Schenck's base hadn't been moved around, nor had William's—great big trees were locking them in the ground—I started to peek at the surveys, recalling what Zach had said to me early on: If we could pinpoint some positions, we might theoretically have a better idea who goes where. Joel and Zach immediately got to work on standing up the Van Sise tablet.

After the men left, I wrote them, hoping for two more mild days before they had to wrap up for the year. Yet what they had accomplished was stupendous. Blank headstones reassembled. Fragments reconnected. Stephen Schenck repaired. Martha Van Sise standing. Jane II well on her way. As was William. And there was so much more to do.

Everybody was invited to come over for another glass of wine in January. Somewhere in my cellar was a bottle of 1990 Chateau Latour. We had something to celebrate, and that would be a good time to pop the cork. But for the time being, I returned to Montauk with my car filled with groceries. Then in December, when Sandy had some doctors visits and we were resettled in Syosset, I started probing again. In the meantime, what work I was doing, I was doing on the computer. And I finally made up my mind to get comfortable with the surveys.

Removing the trees was necessary for the preservation effort. Bill Goldberg, left, and the Brandywine crew.

October 2, 2020, the trees were finally coming down.

The methodical Joel Snodgrass recording his progress.

The tree stump had to be notched for Joel to work with the stone.

Jane Schenck (Jane II under the tree), all set for the next round of drilling.

What prompted me was this: one of the orphaned puzzle pieces with the letters "roy." Examining it closely revealed that it was the top right corner of a headstone. There was no name ending in "roy" on the Frost survey. Nothing on Velsor either. However, the Burckley survey had a Phebe Jane McElroy. Then I took another look at the Frost survey. The ninth name was Phebe Jane McElvoy...a typo! (It wouldn't be the last.)

That got me thinking. If Josephine Frost was transcribing volumes of Wyckoff's field studies and made mistakes, imagine transcribing the Bible. What an imposing task. You're a scribe, working by candlelight, copying page after page; day after day; month after month; year in, year out. Imagine how many mistakes you'd make. Not to be flippant, but one typo and Methuselah lived 900 years.

On December 9, back in Syosset, perusing all the early photos, I saw a picture of the first big tree root I removed that had held two large stones together—one in front of the other. Then I came to a photo of a large fragment on a pallet with "July 5th 1855" etched into it. And a much smaller piece with the letters "Corneli" placed above it. I turned to the surveys to find out who died that day.

No. 27 of 41 on Frost had Cornelia. She was one grave away from Jane II (the grave under the tree). Over to the burying ground I went. The base that I figured was Cornelia's was still in the ground. I went to the pallets, found the heavy stone, carried it over to the base, and sat it on top. They matched.

With so much going on, we had forgotten that the two pieces belonged together. Cornelia was back home. Only, "she" was a "he." Another Frost typo. The Burckley survey said Cornelius. Velsor didn't have anything. It's possible this was one of the headstones he couldn't lift. John Hammond, in his 2007 alphabetical survey, wrote, "Cornelius, 1855." Somebody had reerected it between 1962 and 2007. Somebody had ravaged it again after that. And somebody had buried the pieces one in front of the other to preserve them.

And here's the kicker. Burckley had Cornelius, age 3 months and 4 days, next to James Schenck. There is no James there. He meant Jane. And Cornelius was 76 years, 3 months, and 4 days. Both surveys had March 15, 1846, as the end of Jane/James's life. Two Burckley typos!

The temperature was in the 50s when I returned from the city with Sandy. Taking advantage of the balmy weather, I decided to probe the northwest area that I had cleared earlier in the fall. The pitchfork found some lost footstones and something much larger. I located the border of the object and carefully removed the topsoil with the plastic trowel. Then I used a pickax to clear around the sides and create space for the pry bar. On December 11, 2020, Mary Elizabeth Schenck made her debut.

At first I couldn't read a thing. A little Dawn soap and D/2, and two days later, I could read the inscription. She lived 70 years, 11 months. On the Velsor survey, she lived 7 years, 11 months. How about that, a Velsor typo! (Go ahead, try transcribing the Bible.)

The start of 1890 must have been a complete disaster for the Schencks. They buried three family members that January. Mary Elizabeth died on the 21st. The next day, James Henry died. And three days later, January 25, Phebe Jane McElroy died. There was a bubonic plague pandemic in the 1890s. (Bubonic plague hit the world in three waves from the 1300s to the 1900s, killing millions.) It's probably what claimed them.

By 1893 George Mann was the owner of the Schenck family farmhouse and most of the Schencks had left the area. Mary Eliza Schenck was the last person interred at the family burying ground. She died in 1897, only 28 years old. Perhaps the Black Death took her, too.

Kurt ended up the first year of the pandemic finding a new website that had the Schenck cemetery on it. It's called Peoplelegacy.com. They bill themselves as the first place people should look for genealogical information. There were 28 Schenck family members listed, in descending order from the year they died. It also had the longitude and latitude of the location. Neither Kurt, Zach, or Joel had any idea where they got this information or when it was compiled.

Add this sixth survey to the list of unsolved mysteries.

The reassembly line.

A eureka moment for Zach was the discovery that the Martha Van Sise scripture fit perfectly on the base at the southwest corner of the yard. Our second row.

Stephen Schenck glued and strapped together.

It took Joel three days to get this far with the Jane II headstone.

Zach lining up more of Jane II.

It's a match. Two parts of the Cornelius Schenck headstone.

Unearthing Mary Elizabeth Schenck. Born February 21, 1819. Died January 21, 1890.

CHAPTER 12

We have too many Aarons

New Year's Eve 2021, waiting in my inbox was a message from Bill Hoke. He'd been sending me article after article about all the new technologies driving archaeology into the future. Lidar, from *light detection and ranging*, was one of them. But I'd already been down that road. Sure, in the back of my mind, I would have loved to employ something that might turn up more stones. It simply was beyond my capabilities.

When I opened Hoke's email, instead of a story on some incredible technology, there was a poem:

Haibun

Cemetery Hunting with Mother

She wades into the tall dry grass, waist high in monuments,

Small spiral notebook and stubby pencil in hand,

looking for second and third cousins.

When she finds one where the corn field corners meet,

she writes and talks,

telling me their story, who they were, what they did, where they fit in.

I drive the borrowed car back into Town, dust contrails whirling over the Indiana back roads,

trying to absorb her memories of Uncle Emmanuel

and how he got here in the first place.

Then came three lines Hoke had written in haiku:

we rub their worn-away headstones

with soft pencil and tissue paper

rubbing for a family name

I could never write either form. It's just not me. I write ads—a second-rate art form, which on occasion is first-rate. One of the best practitioners I know is Hoke's best friend, Don Wood. He's a lyricist, and my oldest friend in advertising. As fate would have it, Don would be a major factor in advancing this story.

Don called me from Montreal. It was the 6th of January, 2021. Yelling through his iPhone, he said, "They're breaking into the Capitol!" "Who is?" I asked, shaking off my work gloves. "Trump supporters are storming the Capitol!" "What?" "They're breaking into the Capitol."

I said something to the effect of "Well, that will finally be the end of him. Good riddance. Don, I'm filthy. I'm in the cemetery, and I have to finish up and head back to Montauk. Sorry, I'm running out of daylight. I've got to go. Keep me posted." Before hanging up, he said he wanted to see the cemetery. "Let's get together when the restorers return. Probably May or June. I'll let you know."

On the drive to Montauk, I thought long and hard about his disturbing call. I would be shamefully negligent if I didn't say that this was one of the darkest days in American history.

Sandy and I stayed hunkered down in Montauk during the winter, waiting our turn to get a COVID-19 vaccination. On my trips to Syosset, I was more intent on masking up, putting on rubber gloves, doing my grocery shopping, and hightailing it back to Montauk than sleuthing. In January 2021, 79,000 died, a record for a month. Working remotely was the best I could do. Only once in January did I actually put in some time at the cemetery, and I didn't return again until the end of February, when we went into the city to get vaccinated.

Occasionally I sent out emails trying to keep the ball in the air. I wrote a few to Roger Tollefsen, asking what Southampton did when they had fragments and didn't know where they belonged. I found out that they were cataloged, indicating where they were found and what the nearest marker was, and then stored at a centralized facility in Southampton. As to restored fieldstone markers, Tollefsen suggested we might put them all in one place and create a new marker explaining why they were there. He added that a single plaque with the names of all the deceased might be appropriate.

I contacted Barney at the library to see if he'd made any progress with Dutch Reformed Church records. He told me he had a lead but that the guy wanted to be paid for the information. "It couldn't be much," I said. "He thinks it's worth a lot."

The burial ground January 6, 2021. Bottom left: Mary Elizabeth Schenck, where I found her tablet.

The easternmost row (our row 5) on March 23, 2021, with newly discovered fragments in the background. The largest of which were both halves of the fieldstone Koli dug up in 2019. The June 27, 1804 stone is by the pile of soil. 1804 still hidden underground.

April, 2021. Wildflowers for Martha Boerum Schenck, wife of Andrew Van Sise.

I wrote Zach asking his thoughts on the restoration.

Zach's response:

...Realizing that the damage or loss was so extensive at the Schenck Burying Ground, our strategy was to retrieve and reassemble as many stones as we found, preserve ("palletize") them at or near where they were found as a clue to their final location, and then begin to match them to broken lower segments in the ground, or to family affiliation (i.e., husband next to wife), or to footstones whose initials are also clues to a headstone's location.

In this we've been moderately successful. As you exhume more fragments and more complete stones emerge, we may find locations that better align with the survey. But the larger objective of the work has been met, which is to re-establish the memorialization of the Schenck family at this burying ground through the repair and resurrection of as many headstones as can be retrieved.

By March 19, I was back at the cemetery taking advantage of the fine weather. Spring was in the air. One of the stones had "Aged 41 years, 4 m and 14 days," on it. I couldn't figure out whom it belonged to. Kurt emailed me the answer: 4th entry on the Velsor survey, Aaron Schenck. I looked at the oldest survey, and there were only two Aaron Schencks. Somebody had thrown us a curve. We had three. Where did the third one come from? I was feeling deflated again. "I'll never figure this out," I said to Kurt.

On the 23rd, while I was systematically probing the ground, Zach showed up. He was with a young guy wearing an L.A. Dodgers baseball hat. Zach introduced me to his son, Noah. His eyes were as blue as the hat. The two had met for lunch and were so close to the Schenck site that they'd decided to stop by. Zach was as surprised to see me as I was to see him.

He wrote me afterward: "That was a lucky chance. Noah lives in Brooklyn Heights, and we decided to meet halfway for lunch. Couldn't resist showing him the BG because I'd talked about it. You've been busy! See you later in the spring."

Zach's visit reenergized me. He really cared about this project. He had planned to do a presentation on it at the annual convention of taphophiles—cemetery enthusiasts—who met in different parts of the country each year. There are about 200 members. The pandemic did those gatherings in, too.

I kept at it. By April Fool's Day, I was almost finished probing the quarter acre. Granted, I could go only so deep and I did not do every square inch. And some of the marble had literally melted away, but I had uncovered a lot. On April 14th, I said to Sandy, "Stick a pitchfork in me. I'm done."

Even though I hadn't probed around the root ball under the large maple tree at the entrance to the cemetery yet, I said to the guys, whenever you want to resume, I'm ready. This has been a most gratifying project. Zach replied, "We'll look at our calendars and get it scheduled. I agree... the most gratifying!"

I sent the team photos of other recent finds. Nothing that seemed important at the time. Part of the Mary Schenck footstone and a thick piece of broken marble.

Zach offered up a theory:

After working with you at the site for a while, we've come to the conclusion that this was not an occasional act of vandalism, or deterioration due to falling tree limbs and weather events. The destruction of the site was widespread; headstones were found removed at a considerable distance from their original places, as if lifted up and transported. The cemetery was effectively leveled; nothing remained undamaged. When the adjoining property was excavated and leveled for construction of the brick dormitory, heavy equipment was used. We believe that some deranged individual may have done the damage. May he rest in Hell.

That went on the list of what might have happened here. But I still had trouble buying it. The building is relatively new. Half of the headstones had disappeared between 1902 and the 1940s, before it was built. Furthermore, between 1915 and 1925, the Ku Klux Klan had a major resurgence in the Syosset area. Membership, as stated by Tom Montalbano, was considered "patriotic and commendable" and included not just "farmers, common laborers and the uneducated" but also "some of the most prominent citizens of the area." They were anti-Catholic, anti-Semitic, anti-African American, and anti-immigrant. Who knows, maybe some of them thought the Schenck cemetery was Catholic and had decided to loot it. When I bounced that theory off Kurt, his reaction was the one I prefer.

Kurt wrote:

And then there are people who just simply get a thrill out of breaking things no matter what religion or belief exists. Sometimes it is a dare, sometimes

Some of the last fragments found. The top piece was from Mary Schenck's footstone; the bottom one would turn out to be quite significant.

And this is Sarah Schenck, Aaron's wife. Both headstones were recovered by Don Wood.

The Velsor survey indicates that this belongs to yet another Aaron Schenck.

Don Wood cleaning the pedestal base in our second row.

it is an (often) drunken expression of anger, and sometimes it is borne of stupidity.

Protestants are not in the 20th and 21st centuries known for violent destructive acts as a group, or as a group named as acting on behalf of or by an individual. Protestants evolved from "peaceful protests" and exist that way today, in their true form.

Still, it would be satisfying to know who did this destruction at Schenck and why, but we will never know. I think of it as a random act of destruction much like a random act of kindness, but in the opposite.

The last week in May was the next window for everybody's return. Joel said he had to stop by sooner to see what he needed. He was leaving for a West Coast trip and had to cram in as much as he could before he left. When he told me that, I really didn't think we'd resume in May. Then Zach sent an email zeroing in on May 24 and 25.

One week before the target date, the Town had yet to mow the foot-tall grass. I went to work on Chris (Louis LaRusso was still teaching school). He delivered. By the 21st, the site was cleaned up. And Joel, back from California, happened by just as they were finishing. He sent everyone an email that he needed more C-channels, but they wouldn't be ready in time. We moved things back. June 28 and 29 was the new window. I let Don Wood know.

Also on my mind was wanting to apply for a permit for an October Grand Canyon hike. But the pandemic was still in the way, and half the people in Arizona not only refused to wear masks but also refused to get vaccinated. I wondered how they'd feel if they were in surgery and the doctors and nurses didn't wear masks or latex gloves?

Don came to Montauk for a visit and then joined Zach, Joel, and me in Syosset. Kurt had to bail. After the requisite introductions, Don dove right in. The guy is game. He's worked with glassblowers, coached peewee and college ice hockey, taught lyric writing, and wrote the lyrics for some of the most famous advertising jingles of the day. He's a wordsmith; a humanitarian; a superb photographer; and, as his name might imply, a woodworker. Both Zach and Joel really got a kick out of my Canadian friend lying on his side, working on one of the pedestal bases.

Then I asked him to dig up two paired headstone pieces in our last row, right next to the restored Aaron Schenck. We marked the spot, and he placed the large marble stones on a pallet.

Next Don went to work in the fourth row, digging up a headstone without a base. When he exposed it and I looked at the bottom, I thought it might fit on one of the tabs in the second row. We carried it over. Close but no cigar. Then we tried the tab next to the two slabs Don had put on the pallet. A match!

The inscription said, "In Memory of Sarah." I couldn't read the rest, so I went home and got the surveys, and in the Velsor report, the fourth, fifth, and six entries were Aaron, followed by another Aaron, and then "In Memory of Sarah, wife of Aaron." The headstones Don dug up found their Velsor homes. According to that survey, Aaron's family was finally back together again. To which Don replied, "Can you dig it!"

Zach and Joel, who had been working both together and apart repairing Jane under the tree as well as other markers, were duly impressed with the new finds. Even more so when I showed them all the pieces I had put together for what was now Aaron III.

I said to Joel that he was going to need to spray some WD-40 on his knees from all the bending he had to do.

The team managed another half day together before we had to pack it in. It was brutally hot and taking its toll on Zach. As much as I wanted to continue, it wasn't fair to any of the guys.

During the summer, on trips back and forth to Syosset, I stopped by many historic cemeteries in East Hampton and Southampton Towns. There were always damaged headstones, but nothing was bashed to bits like Cemetery 104.

However, I wasn't the only one touring old burial grounds that summer. On July 13, while I was putting in some time in Syosset, a guy named Rob showed up. He said he was a friend of Zach's and had heard he was working here. Rob went by the moniker Musicguy and had attended some of Zach's historic cemetery tours. I still can't figure out how he got wind of this. Zach didn't tell him. He was quite complimentary and curious.

As soon as he left, I made another discovery. The midsection of the second Aaron Schenck headstone fit perfectly on the tab right next to William Schenck's

The bottom two elements were not part of the third Aaron's tombstone.

The midsection of the second Aaron Schenck finding its mate.

Zach and Joel fitting Aaron Schenck III back together. The oldest of the Aarons, he was born November 7, 1783, and died September 15, 1871.

From the rear, Aaron Schenck II looks like a sculpture.

marker. The Frost and Burckley surveys show that's where Aaron II should be. The top of his stone was braced on C-channels not that far away. Burckley recorded only one Aaron Schenck (spelled "Aron," another typo), not three. And as I mentioned earlier, the old church records would reveal that Aaron and Sarah had no kids. Where did the other Aaron headstone come from? Why was he next to Aaron and Sarah?

I suppose someone just figured that was where he belonged, reunited with his parents. And this is really curious and took forever to figure out: Even though the first Aaron and Aaron II are in different locations, they're a duplicate of the same headstone. They both have the same inscription. Only you can barely read "41 years, 4 months and 14 days" on the first Aaron the team restored.

In 2024, when I received the official DAR survey, just to double-check, I looked up the Aarons. Again, there were only two. The first one said, "d. Mar. 3, 1863; Ae. 41-4-14. (Stone fallen.)" Could it be that somebody ordered a replacement headstone, thinking the fallen stone was a goner, and then, like most everything else at the site, it got lost in the shuffle?

Kurt, always upbeat, was very impressed that the second Aaron had come together.

He wrote:

Great match. Seems like there is always something new coming to the light. Will be difficult to decide when to stop - or should I say if to stop.

I knew that this couldn't go on forever. We were missing too many pieces. And besides, it was getting costly. But when to stop? Certainly not yet.

Barney arranged a cameo visit on July 27. Before his arrival, I asked Louis LaRusso if the site could be mowed. He wasn't sure. So I schlepped my lawn mower from Montauk and cut the grass myself. Wouldn't you know it? The Highway Department showed up when I finished.

It had been a long time between Barney visits. He was amazed at the progress and said, "If nothing else was done, it's a home run!" Little did any of us know that the next time he returned, it would look different yet again.

He asked when the guys were returning. "September," I said, "after the weather cools down."

Found another needle in the haystack!

CHAPTER 13

We have too many rows

Alone in Syosset, near the end of the day, August 9, 2021, I was walking around the burying ground, just taking it all in. A footstone caught my eye. It had the initials PJM, Phebe Jane McElroy.

I remembered her from the typo on the Frost survey. This tiny stone, all by itself, maybe five inches tall, had somehow missed the sledgehammer. Across from it was nothing more than a broken base a few inches out of the ground. The width of the base was the same as the width of the "roy" fragment lying over on a pallet. Phebe's little footstone led to her headstone.

It took a few minutes to remind myself of the self-evident. If I could find Phebe on the earliest survey, I would have a good idea who was buried in the vandalized graves on each side of her. Back to the house, ninth listing, there she was, Phebe. The eighth was Henry. Seventh, Jane. The one after Phebe, No. 10, was Martha Van Sise. The Burckley survey had 11 people in the first row, with Martha Van Sise No. 1 and Phebe second. Jane and Henry were 3 and 4—somehow reversed from the Frost survey.

So these two surveys, taken in opposite directions, both had Phebe next to Martha Van Sise. Jane and Henry were next to her, too, all in the first row, our second row. Under my breath, I said, "Uh-oh, we have too many rows!"

The next mind-bender was that the order of the surveys never quite lined up. Twenty names from the Frost survey were missing on the Burckley list. And headstones were moved around. Fortunately, Burckley did tell us there were three rows. However, the way we'd found the site made figuring out who went where impossible. Today, four children's markers separate Phebe and Martha Van Sise. Who did that? What goes where? Which stone is in the right place, Phebe's or Martha's?

What's left of the kids' memorials is in shambles, all unidentifiable. Which survey do we restore to? Is anything where it's supposed to be? I felt like I was stuck in the old Abbott and Costello routine, "Who's on first. What's on second. I Don't Know is on third."

Give credit to the recordkeepers. If it weren't for their surveys, we'd have no clues whatsoever. To be sure, the site was looted, damaged, and repaired between 1902 when Wyckoff walked it and 1932, when the Daughters of the American Revolution were there. It was damaged and repaired again between then and Burckley's 1940s list, and once again before Velsor's 1962 visit, and then again by the time Hammond came over in 2007. And after that, it was destroyed and left for dead.

Over the years, every time somebody tried to repair it, it was done incorrectly. The restorers did what we did: made educated guesses. Along the way, somebody decided to put all the kids[11] between Phebe and Martha. And even if we had all the missing headstones, we still couldn't re-create what Wyckoff saw. Simply because we don't know how many rows there were. Or how many graves were in each row. Or if he recorded all the names from left to right.

All I could think to do was make a detailed map of every row, gravestone, and footstone and include the names, dates, and numbers from the different surveys.

Back to the cemetery I went, approaching it in the only way possible, from the southwest, photographing everything from left to right, row by row. Then I took a 3-foot-by-14-inch sheet of brown wrapping paper and, following the photos, drew a map and added all the pertinent info. By 10 p.m., I was done and drew lines from where the headstones were to where they needed to go. In the morning, I returned to the cemetery to see if I was right.

All the headstones in our first row were supported on braces. According to the wrapping paper map, Jane and Henry had to be moved back one row and to the right. I looked at the bottom of Jane's marker and then the top of the broken tab next to Phebe, which was in two pieces when Kurt and I first saw it and Joel mended

[11] The 1912 Frost transcript of Wyckoff's field studies did have four infants buried next to each other in what I believed was the first row—Frost 3, 4, 5 and 6: Ann, age 3 months, 23 days; Elbert, age 5 months, 1 day; Martha J., age 2 months, 18 days; and Nelson, age 4 months, 18 days. They were all listed alphabetically in the 1932 DAR survey, but in the 1940s when Burckley recorded his survey row by row, their headstones were gone. Ann reappeared in 1962 and survived through Hammond's 2007 visit. She's gone today. Hammond also lists an Elbert 1815 (date of death), but that date doesn't match the two Elberts on the Frost Survey—1845 and 1867. Today, only pieces remain of the four children's graves—from left to right in the first row, they are in positions 11–14. Frost also lists five other children buried next to each other—Frost 17–21—all children of Simeon Schenck and Mary Darling, whose headstones have vanished. They range in age from infants to 10 years old: Juliette, Harriet A., Mary Emily, Jane, and Simeon. None of their gravestones survived, nor are they on any other survey. Simeon and Mary had eight more children. There are two other children buried in the cemetery, Frost 30, Jane Louisa Ellison, age 2 days, and Frost 40, Louisa Lewis, age 12 years. Both are in the 1932 DAR survey and have disappeared after that.

Phebe Jane McElroy's undamaged footstone.

I drew a map to show where every stone was, and where they should be according to each survey. With so many gravestones missing, there was a lot of guesswork. Phebe's footstone is in the white circle on the right-hand page.

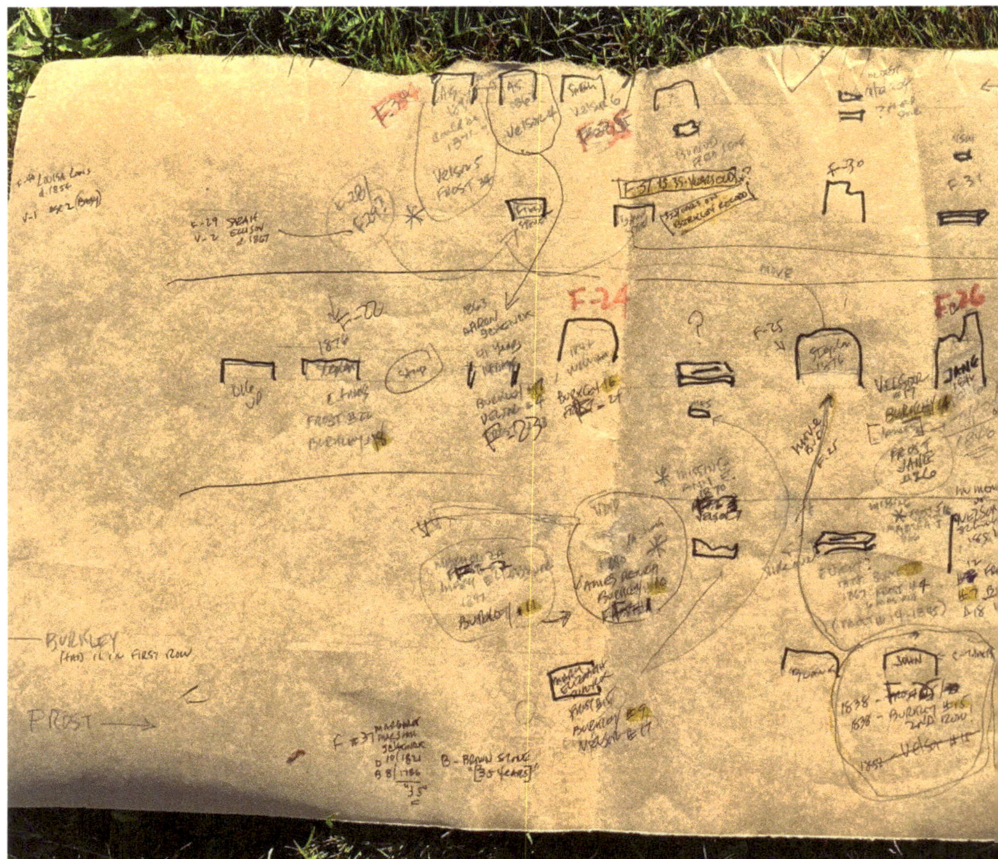

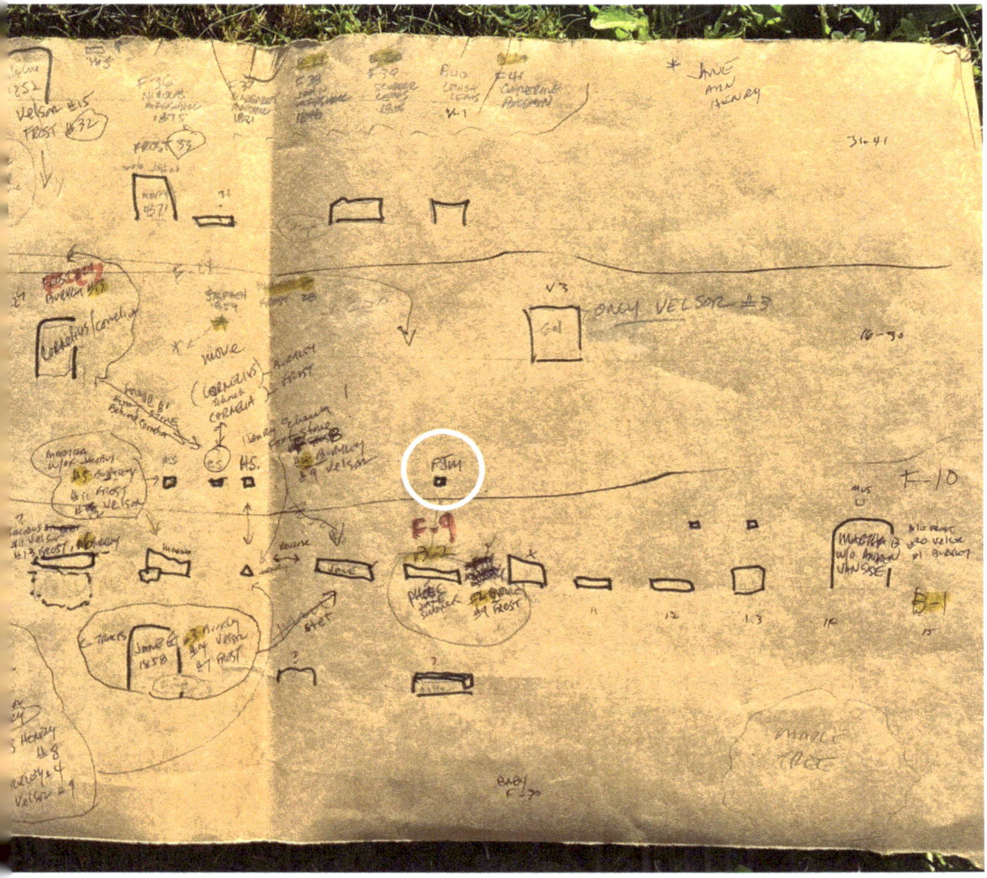

We had Henry and Jane in the wrong place. They had to be moved back to what looked to be the real first row.

Henry should go to the flag on the left, Jane to the one on the right. The fragment in the foreground, we would learn, belongs to the next gravesite, Phebe McElroy.

it. It seemed like they would match. To prove it, I would have to lift Jane's enormous stone up and out of the C-channels and carry it to the base. Nothing doing. That would be a two-man job, maybe three. The 2-inch-thick marble easily weighed 80 pounds.

Just as Phebe's footstone led to her headstone, Henry's footstone led to his. Using Joel's red marking flags to show where the stones belonged, I took some pictures and sent them to the team.

Joel wrote back:

Now that is really impressive. I'm going to start calling you jig-saw master! lol!

The map showed that the two Stephen Schencks needed to be switched. That John, off by himself in his own last row, needed to be moved forward one row and placed next to his wife, Mary, and his parents. I dug up his headstone, a 100-pounder, and wrestled it onto 2 x 4s. The two Stephens were easier to move around.

September 20–22 was the next window for the team to resume. Once again Kurt couldn't make it. Don was in Montreal. The plan was for Joel to finish his repairs, and then we'd start moving things around. He and Zach continued working their magic on William.

When the second Aaron was clamped and vertical, Joel and Zach turned their attention to the third Aaron. Which was another painstaking repair.

Finally, the three of us moved Jane next to Phebe, in what I thought was the first row. The large headstone fit squarely on the tab. Joel glued the pieces together. Then he and Zach repaired the June 27, 1804, fieldstone, followed by Sarah, wife of Aaron. An astonishing amount of work was done, and there was still more to do.

Near the end of the second day, with Joel's approval, I carried the three James Henry fragments to the very first spot in the first row—the No. 1 position, according to Frost—and set them on the ground.

As if on a mission, I dug up a very large, nameless, partially repaired base from the old front row that Kurt had once worked on (see page 66). We needed to find a new place for it. When I looked at it carefully, it seemed to be the same thickness as the James Henry pieces. What the heck, I dragged it over to the three fragments.

What happened next was not one but three incredible moments. First a very thick fragment that didn't seem significant when I found it on the other side of

The tape shows drilling and gluing points.

At last, William was back in the ground.

Jane Schenck, once again in her 1940s location next to Phebe. The 1912 Frost survey has Henry in this spot and Jane one to the left.

From the northeast corner looking southwest, the June 27, 1804, headstone is on the pallet, with Aaron III. The bottom of Aaron's marker has three pieces of tape. His wife, Sarah, has two.

No ordinary fieldstone, it appears to have been quarried.

the yard—a good 30 feet from where I was standing—popped into my head. I retrieved it, and it turned out to be the linchpin connecting the three small James Henry elements to the much larger base. Joel and Zach were stunned. Without that one small piece of stone, we never would have figured out that the top and bottom connected.

Second, there was a large piece of marble with a flat, tapered bottom over on the pallets. I never could find a home for it. Due to its distinctive shape, Zach called it "New Hampshire." I carried it over, and it fit perfectly in the pedestal base Joel had repaired. He smiled. I was on a roll—and not done yet.

At the very last moment, I turned to the guys and said, "Just for grins…" and walked over to a large dark headstone off by itself on the north side of the yard. It was still at the location where we'd found it. Dug only a few inches into the ground. I pulled it up and placed it next to the last piece of marble from the old first row. Joel and Zach were in disbelief. So was I. They matched.

The spirits of the Schencks had taken over the restoration.

The following morning, Zach and Joel managed to drive 75 miles from Sag Harbor and 10 miles from Huntington and arrive before I could walk 300 yards across the street. They were up to their elbows in repairs when I got there. We talked it over and decided we should put the last headstone from the night before at the southern end of the second row to fill it out.

The stone was unreadable. On the Frost survey after the "New Hampshire" stone—which might very well have belonged to Elbert—came two children. What was there was much too large for them. I thought about moving two of the children over to conform to Frost, but which two? It was pure guesswork, and with so many missing gravestones, what was the point?

I was finally at peace with the fact that we would never be able to get everything right and the entire project when done would be an homage to all the Schencks. (A conclusion Zach and company had reached much earlier.)

As you would expect, we didn't finish that day, and Zach and Joel were back at it on October 27–28, to "button things up for the winter." They brought along a stranger, Kurt Kahofer. It was so good to see him again.

Interred, unknown. The piece that resembles New Hampshire is in the foreground.

Frost and Burckley crisscross here, indicating that this is Elbert. But which one? Both surveys have different birth and death dates. One for an adult and one for a child.

James Henry Schenck died January 22, 1890. Age 35 years, 4 months, and 12 days. The third fragment down on the left was the missing link reuniting James Henry's headstone.

Placed where we found it, this badly eroded marble stone sat alone on the north side of the yard.

Final match of the day—September 21, 2021. The mate to the eroded stone above was the last removed from our old first row.

Although I've not said much about the desecrated footstones, it was a major victory every time we were able to restore one.

In all our restorations, we used a combination of epoxy and pins where necessary.

CHAPTER 14

The widowmaker blockage

With all the new work, and finishing up the old, Kurt arrived just in the nick of time. While Joel and Zach moved around large stones and slid them into freshly widened holes, Kurt dove into pointing and mortaring.

Joel was full of surprises and would soon find out he was in for one. From some deep recess in his trailer, out came a pair of bright orange straps. He worked them under James Henry, adjusted them to arm's length, slid them up to both his and Zach's elbows, and then locked his hand to his wrist. On his command, both men lifted the enormous slab with their forearms and jockeyed it about six feet between some pallets, to what we believed was its original position on the Frost survey. Beads of sweat punctuating their foreheads. Then Joel lifted his end up while Zach guided the bottom into the ground. Once it was in position, he began the laborious process of joining the pieces together.

What is frustrating is that James Henry Schenck, who died in 1890, is listed first on the Frost survey and is not listed last in the first row on the Burckley survey. Burckley recorded the graves in the opposite direction, from right to left, and Mary "Elizabether"[12] (Mary Eliza), the last to be buried in the cemetery, is in his last position. James Henry is second-to-last. Which survey is correct, Frost or Burckley? Was the order inadvertently reversed on the Frost survey? Did she make a mistake transcribing Wyckoff's field notes? Or did Burckley get it wrong? It sure would make sense, though, that Mary Eliza would be in the last spot, not James Henry. On the other hand, it's just as likely that somebody found the headstones pulled from the ground and put them back in the wrong places and that's what Burckley recorded. Or maybe it's none of the above. So many things just don't add up.

The pinning and gluing of Cornelius, son of Nicholas and Sytie (a.k.a. Cynthia or Catharine) Emons, was finally finished. He rests in the second row, one grave from his wife, Jane Boerum (Jane II, under the tree).

[12] That's how she's spelled on the survey.

On Jane's left is their son John, born August 20, 1808, died March 4, 1838. And to his left is their son William—remember him? And again, to his left is another son, Aaron (Aaron II), born October 17, 1821, died March 3, 1863. Then comes another son, Stephen, born March 29, 1824, died May 12, 1876.

Cornelius and Jane had five other children, Nicholas, who died August 29, 1882 (burial location and birthdate unknown); Philip Ellis, born on my birthday, different century—March 15, 1806, died April 6, 1896. (His wife is buried in Bayville; perhaps he is, too.) Next comes Elizabeth; then Margaret, wife of John Marshall; and finally Sarah, wife of James Ellison.

There is one unidentified pedestal base that found its way between John and Stephen. I doubt that it belongs there, but there it will remain.

After placing and then tamping soil around the unidentified headstone that filled out the second row, Joel went back to work on Aaron III—the oldest of the Aarons and last to be found.

Then he turned his attention to what we believe was the Jacobus marker, the melting marble headstone that dried out on a plywood board and was miraculously saved. No wording survived. Jacobus died January 17, 1873, age 81 years, 7 months, 22 days, and based on Burckley's survey, he should be one grave over from his wife, Martha.

Martha died May 19, 1877, age 83 years, 7 months, and 29 days. We would find only two pieces of her headstone to place on the scripture-engraved base. One piece with "Mar" and one with "age 83 years, 7 months and 29 days."

That was followed by the next big repair, Sarah Ellison, a daughter of Cornelius and Jane. She was 18 years old when she passed away—two years after the end of the Civil War. A little luck led us to the tab of her headstone.

As things were winding down for the day, there was one other piece of unfinished business. Based on my map, I dug up the headstone of John Schenck who was off by himself on the far side of the burying ground. He was the first son of the "d. June 27,1804" John Schenck.

This third-generation East Woods farmer was born July 20, 1774; died March 2, 1852; and had to be moved next to his wife, Mary, in row 4. It would take the four of us to carry his massive stone.

James Henry, being moved to what I believed was position No. 1 on the Frost survey.

"On 3! Watch your fingers, Zach."

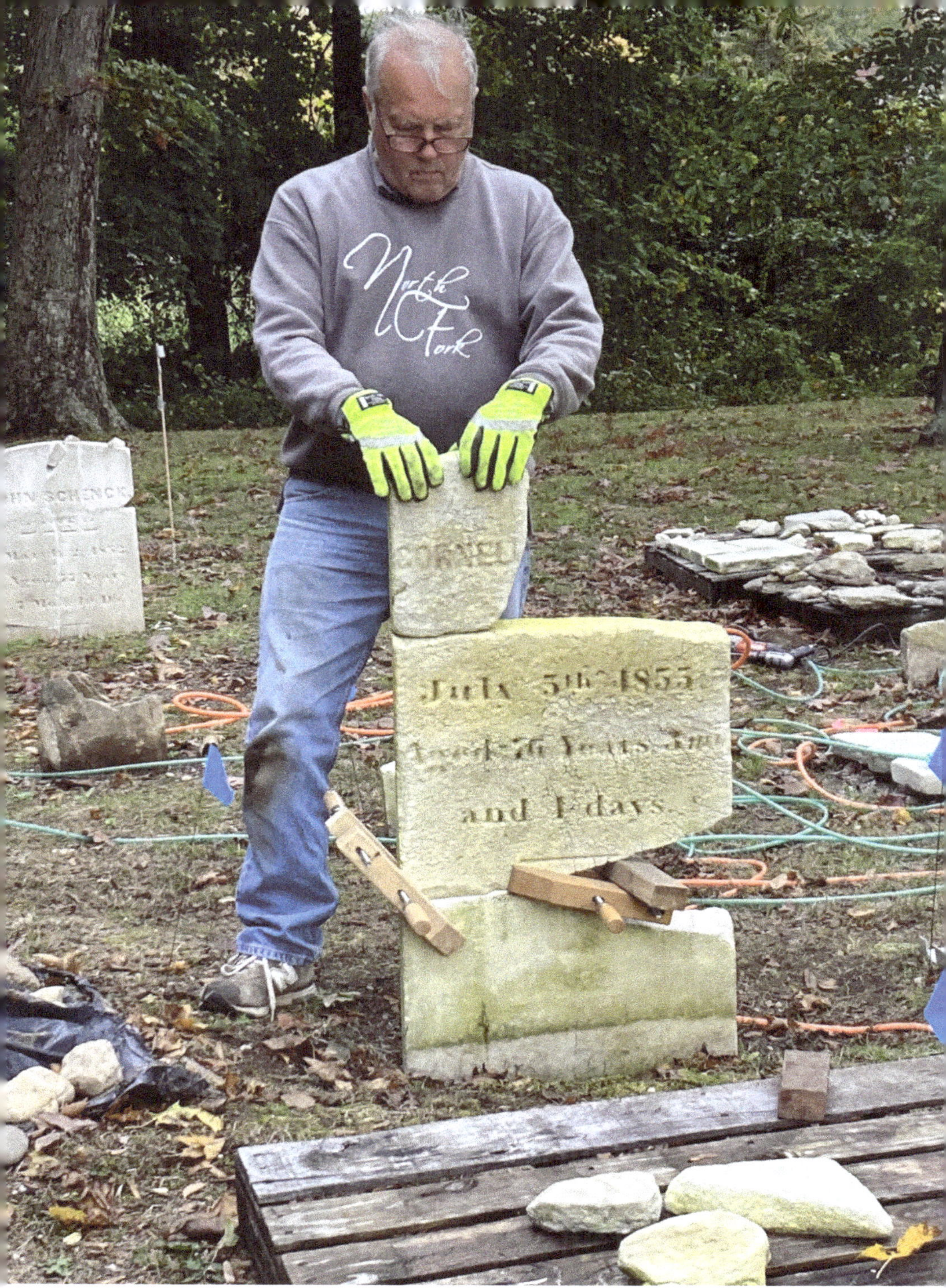

Zach Studenroth finishing up the last of the repairs of the Cornelius stone.

Possibly Jacobus Schenck, born May 26, 1791, died January 17, 1873.

All that's left of Martha, wife of Jacobus.

The base for John Schenck's massive headstone.

Sarah, wife of James Ellison, was the last piece Joel would work on that year.

Joel Snodgrass showing off his work to his wife, Alice.

When Kurt and I dug the hole for John, my shovel hit a large piece of marble. Kurt and I exposed the top of it, and it looked like it might fit the Sutter base in the first row. Joel handed me his tape measure to check. No luck. So we placed John in the ground next to Mary and I told everybody I would dig up the fragment later on and try to find a home for it.

Believe it or not, Mr. Ripley, that winter when I dug it up, it turned out to be the base of John's headstone. The wrapping paper map was spot-on. I would have to somehow get John's headstone out of the ground to prove it. Due to its size and weight, this would require makeshift 2 x 4 scaffolding, a couple of long shovels, the pry bar, a lot of leverage, and all my might.

Given the amount of surgery needed to put the Schenck family site back together, the place looked more like the Joel Snodgrass sculpture garden than a graveyard. And of all the pieces of sculpture, Joel's favorite was Sarah, wife of James Ellison. She was born March 8, 1849, died September 19, 1867.

As we were wrapping up for the day, I overheard Joel say he was about to go in for previously scheduled surgery. He suffered from atrial fibrillation. I was startled. He sure looked like the picture of health to me.

On November 6, a few days before his procedure, Joel came by to pick up his clamps and move around a headstone or two. He brought along his lovely wife, Alice. They were planning a trip to Paris for their daughter's wedding. Their son Koli was also making plans to go to the altar. I took a photo of the happy parents.

For the short period of time they were there, Joel had to do more heavy lifting to prevent Henry and Jacobus from getting damaged. Both stones had settled in such a way that they wouldn't have lasted the winter, collapsing under their own weight.

We said our goodbyes. I was about to head off on a mid-November, eight-day Grand Canyon trek. I applied for the permit on July 1, saying the heck with the Arizonans, I needed to take a hike.

My former art director, and a great friend for more than 40 years, wanted to join me. He lives in Minneapolis, and just before the trip, he was in New York, staying with me. I brought him over to the cemetery to show off the work. He took one look at the damage and said, "Put your Stephen King hat on for a moment, Rav, and I'll tell you what happened here."

My friend, a jaded ex-Catholic who was thrown out of Catholic school for hitting a nun in the head with a snowball, unflinchingly said, "The nuns did it!"

He went into elaborate detail about the horrible treatment he had experienced at the hands of the nuns—starting when he was a five-year-old in the brutal Minnesota winters. Then he segued into the hatred between the different factions of Christianity, explaining that there's an ongoing argument over which is the supreme Christian religion. "The Catholics and Protestants fought a 30-year war over it," he said.

My friend is willing to wager that the nuns made "the little angels" dig up those Protestant gravestones and break them. So you can add that to the list of theories on what happened here.

Just before boarding the flight back from the Grand Canyon, I sent Joel a text, asking how his heart procedure went. When I landed in New York, I was taken aback by his reply. It had never happened. During his presurgery tests, the doctors rushed him into the OR, informing him that he had a "widowmaker" blockage. They managed to get a stent in him and saved his life.

The bottom line is this: At any time during his backbreaking work that fall—including his visit with Alice—Joel could have had a massive heart attack and fallen over dead. He said he would be out of commission for quite some time. The AFib would have to wait, and so would the cemetery.

It was a few days before Thanksgiving. I sent him flowers and well wishes. He had a lot to be thankful for. We all did. Joel is a rare breed.

CHAPTER 15

Digging up the past

Joel would go on to have his originally scheduled procedure and was back in action by June 2022. In the interim, the Burying Ground Preservation Group and I had our annual wine-tasting celebration at my old farmhouse in mid-January. Joel had to go easy on the wine and everything else in life. His daughter's plans were pushed back. Koli's marriage was, too. But he was happy to relax and reflect on the Schencks and how they had brought the four of us together.

Kurt was busy caring for his mom. That became a full-time job. Zach was fully immersed in the Sag Harbor Historical Society and his dance card was always full. I wanted to do something to move the project along, so I contacted Barney at the library to schedule another podcast and to take him up on his offer to fly a drone over the cemetery and photograph everything from above. But Barney's mother was ill and would soon pass away. Then the poor man had back problems and was hospitalized. Everything we scheduled was put on hold. He's still dealing with chronic back pain.

The best I could do was to put together a punch list. A few fragments here and there that I'd found homes for needed to be glued in place. The base of John Schenck had to be attached and his tablet put back in the ground. "New Hampshire" had fallen over, so that needed fixing. There was also a stone with scripture attached to a small tree stump. I dug it up and with it another piece of the same stone. They had to be rejoined. We'll never know whom it belonged to. What remains of the inscription is barely visible.

The oldest of the Aarons also needed more work. I found a few more pieces for it. And another small piece of Jane II needed Joel's attention.

On the pallets, off to the east, were Emma Jane (daughter of James R. and Sarah Ellison and wife of Charles Wanser), who died January 15, 1870, age 18. The same age as her mom.[13] Her headstone was a work in progress. As was that of Catharine Baldwin, who passed away September 3, 1854, age 34 years.

[13] Something isn't right here. Mom was born 1849, died 1867. Frost says daughter Emma was born 1852, died 1870.

Another disaster. Another unknown monument to put back together.

More pieces for the headstone of Steven Schenck, born July 15, 1784, died December 22, 1859.

Don Wood is holding one of the pieces of this unknown marker. (Possibly Margaret Schenck Marshall.)

NSM, the footstone of Nicholas S. Marshall.

Catharine's name is missing. Only "Age 34" and some scripture remain. We could identify her because she is the only person on all the surveys who died at that age. Baldwin was probably a surname from a second marriage. I sent the punch list to the team.

Don Wood stopped by for a few days in March for a tour of the site and took a bunch of pictures. While he was there, I made a few more discoveries, which had to be added to the list.

One was the top right-hand corner of Sarah, wife of James Ellison. Another was some large fragments Zach found on the northwest corner that were still lying where he'd found them. They matched one of the Stephen Schenck markers 10 yards away. C-channels were needed for them.

Mary Elizabeth's long-undisturbed footstone "MES" guided us to where her headstone would stand. More C-channels had to be ordered for her.

And over by the eighteenth-century part of the yard, in the third row, is a marble stub I found a few elements for. But nothing indicating who he or she was. Since the base was near so many restored fieldstones, I'll hazard a guess and say it was Margaret, buried near her parents, Nicklas (Nicholas) Schenck and Sytie Emons.

It's not a bad guess. There's a footstone one grave away with the letters NSM, Nicholas S. Marshall—her son. Nicholas was born March 25, 1808, and died June 30, 1875. Nothing is left of his headstone but an empty pedestal. According to the *Documented History of the Dutch Congregation of Oyster Bay,* John Marshall, a schoolteacher, was his dad. He died September 4, 1846, age 71, before East Woods was renamed Syosset. Stoutenbergh says he is interred "at the farm." Which means one space over from Nicholas should be John Marshall, right? There is no sign of a gravestone. I probed everywhere.

Unfortunately for my guesswork, Frost has all the Marshalls at the very end of her survey. Frost 36, 37, and 38 out of 41. Which would place that family in row 4, one row away.

Of course, given that everything has been moved around over time, I could be right about Margaret's headstone and wrong about her location. Margaret is not recorded on any survey after Frost. Her marker disappeared sometime between 1902 and 1932. The DAR found John and Nicholas in 1932. Burckley found only John's marker—row 3, No. 3 of three, his last row. The Marshall name disappeared after that.

Continuing with the updated repair list, the Martha Van Sise footstone, "MVS," needed aluminum braces. As did one of the children's partially restored headstones in the front row. I also found the top right-hand corner of the James Henry stone. It needed to be reattached.

Throughout the project, Mark Kurnicki and I stayed in contact. It had been a while since he'd examined our work. I asked him to take a look. He was more than complimentary, as was every one of the Mercy First employees whom I ran into on the way to and from the cemetery. Mark walked around the graves and then turned to me and said that the big maple tree at the entrance to the site should come down and offered to do it. He got no argument from me. Some of the branches looked like they might fall on Martha Van Sise, and there's no question the tree would spawn many more maples that would ultimately take root and cause problems.

Mark's men cut the tree to about four feet off the ground and took away the wood. The large stump was beyond them. I needed to hire Brandywine to grind it up. That wouldn't happen until the fall.

When the Burying Ground Preservation Group saw the picture of the site without the tree, they were surprised and amazed. The quarter-acre lot was a world apart from what they'd seen three years earlier.

Zach wanted to hold off on the next, and hopefully last, of the repairs until the fall to avoid the summer heat, but Joel had some time in his schedule and decided on June 6 and 7. His main reason: He had Koli around to keep him from doing anything "stupid." (Joel's word, not mine.)

The Snodgrass team took care of most of the items on the punch list. But not all. And some things I had missed. For instance, Henry Schenck's headstone was on a pallet waiting for the bottom of his base to be excavated and reset and one more element to be glued to it.

There's more to say about Henry, but first it's time to revisit Garret Nostrand, whose headstone kept appearing and disappearing on the surveys.

Garret (also spelled Garrit in the Dutch Reformed Church records) died July 10, 1843, "in the 87th year of his age." Convent Road was once named Nostrand Avenue. The Stoutenbergh book says Nostrand "is bd. on the farm at East Woods (now Syosset) and the monument is the only one with an inscription."

When I read "the only one with an inscription," I wondered if there was another cemetery, a Nostrand family cemetery, somewhere on the Church property? And more than half a century later, after the Sisters of Mercy bought the land, Garret's headstone was stumbled upon and moved over to the Schenck site? Or was he buried with the Schencks before they had proper markers?

It's not like headstones were stamped out by machine. On one of his visits, Zach pointed out something quite unique about almost all the Schenck tablets. The typography started and ended at the edges of the marble stones. Which raises a two-part question: If none of the monuments had any inscriptions in 1843, or at least any that were observed, were most of the Schenck gravestones made by the same hand? And were they made en masse, after 1843, and subsequently replaced wooden crosses or unmarked fieldstones?

To answer that, we needed to know who made the monuments and look at their maps and files. All we know is that Daniel Sutter made one of them. And he was born in 1843. Another mystery to unravel.

Yes, I'm a slow study. During the course of this project, I finally learned that it's much easier to dig with my head than my hands. Probing the internet instead of the ground, I came across Henry Schenck's name in a gruesome article, "The Nostrand Murder," by local historian Tom Montalbano.

On Saturday night, January 21, 1871, another Garret Nostrand, Garret Wort (Wortman) Nostrand, originally from White Hall, who was living in the Nostrand farmhouse across the street from the Schencks, was at a local tavern called the Syosset Hotel. The popular watering hole for farmers and railroad workers was about three-quarters of a mile away.

The "burly" 57-year-old Nostrand, known for frequent disputes with neighbors, got into a heated argument with two other men over sheep getting on his land. When he left for home, he was followed by the men. "On Sunday morning at about 8:00 a.m., Mr. Nostrand's neighbor, Henry Schenck, found his lifeless, bludgeoned body, partially covered in snow halfway between the Syosset Hotel and the Nostrand Home on Convent Road." The murderers were tracked down by their boot prints in the snow. You can Google the gory details if you like.

I bring this story up because, other than the surveys, the Stoutenbergh records and a relatively recent book called *Syosset People and Places*, by John Delin, this is the only mention of any of the Syosset Schencks I've come across. All Delin wrote

Mark's men removed the large maple at the entrance to the cemetery.

Garret Nostrand, born 1756; baptized June 26, 1757; died July 10, 1843.

Koli and Joel putting the finishing touches on Henry Schenck.

Henry, one year later.

Joel's favorite, Sarah, wife of James Ellison, pinned, glued, and finished.

June 24, 2022, the marble headstone of John Schenck hoisted into position one last time.

was, "Before the Manns the land was owned by Stefan Schenck." (This Schenck died in 1876. There is no record of when the farm was sold to Mann.)

There is also an 1873 Syosset map, shown in the appendix, that shows the houses of H. Schenck; J. Schenck; S. Schenck (my home); and, near Cold Spring Harbor, B.H. Schenck.

A few days after Joel and Koli left, I drove up to Boston to visit some friends. Wouldn't you know it: The first thing we did was tour old burying grounds—a busman's holiday.

I learned that because space was at a premium, people were often buried one on top of the other, two and three deep. And when it rained, the top corpse, only a few inches underground, often became exposed, causing cholera epidemics. And that it was Paul Revere who declared that all burials must be six feet deep. I also discovered that in all of Boston, there was nothing that even came close to the sheer destruction of the Schenck family site.

Joel and Koli were back on June 24, sleeves rolled up, and stood up the 125-to-150-pound John Schenck marker. They used a tripod to hoist the monument, and when they were finished, I believe I had seen every tool of the stone surgeon trade.

John now stands side by side with wife Mary again, the longest-lived of them all. Mary was one month and 10 days into her 99th year. Along with attaching the base of John's headstone, Joel and Koli checked off virtually everything on the punch list, with the exception of repairing Emma Jane and Catharine Baldwin. That would have to wait for another day.

Back home in Montauk, with time to kill before my next hike, I stopped by the home of some acquaintances. Their daughter told me they were at Shagwong, a popular local pub. I drove over to say hello. The lady of the couple, Lisa Grenci, is part Dutch. When I told her that I was restoring a Dutch Reformed cemetery in Syosset, she flipped out. She's obsessed with tracking down old documents and asked me to send her the names of some of the people. Henry Schenck was one of them. The next day, I got a free pass to Ancestry.com in my inbox and a link to Henry's life.

Jacobus Nicholassen Schenck (son of Nicholas and Sytie Emons) and Martha Boerum were Henry's parents. Henry had married Phebe Jane Bennet. After Henry died, Phebe remarried and became a McElroy. That explains why Henry and Phebe are next to each other on the Frost survey. It doesn't, however, explain why Jane is between Henry and Phebe on the Burckley survey. But I'll get to that. Mary Eliza was Henry's daughter. James Henry his son. They're all in row 1.

I was positively thrilled to learn about this. At that time, I didn't know that the Stoutenbergh book existed or anything about anyone in the yard. This was the first I learned who was related to whom. And sent the information to the restoration team; Barney; Mark; Louis LaRusso; Chris Sabellico; his replacement at Parks, Jeanne Gatto; and Parks Commissioner Joseph Pinto. We had brought not only the cemetery back to life but Henry, too. Everybody was moved.

My friend kept sending me more information. I joined Ancestry.com for the trial period but quickly grew disillusioned. It wanted to help me find out about my ancestry, not the Schencks', and I had a hard time navigating the site. Fortunately, the discovery of *Documented History of the Dutch Congregation of Oyster Bay* about a year later provided the things I had been searching for. It turns out that Henry Schenck actually had two wives: first Jane Vanderwater and then Phebe Jane Bennet. So that's why Jane and Phebe are both buried next to Henry.

Mary Elizabeth was Henry's sister. Nelson was his brother, and Martha Boerum was another sister, and she married Andrew Van Sise. And Henry had two other brothers, Simeon and Elbert.

The first 16 people on the Frost survey include all these names. Alas, if we had only known how many were in each row, we really could have done justice to the Schenck family.

I took a picture of the cemetery from the same angle as the restoration team's photo at our first meeting. It was astonishing to see the difference, and I sent the before-and-after snapshots to the crew. Kurt shared them with his sisters, and one of them sent back a ghostly black-and-white artist's rendering he forwarded to me. It was an ethereal, almost translucent photograph of people by their graves. There were a man and a woman dressed in their wedding day finery, a little girl walking a dog, a young man and woman facing onlookers, a lady in profile with a parasol sitting on her headstone, an innocent young toddler sitting on the ground, and another little girl off all by her lonesome.

This was a beautiful metaphor for the Schencks—early American farmers who lived hard lives in hard times. What was done to their memorial is outrageous!

John Schenck, born July 20, 1774, died March 2 1852, alongside his wife Mary, born August 18, 1773, died September 28, 1871.

Mary's repaired footstone survived. John's has not.

CHAPTER 16

The missing Church files

In mid-September 2022, I got word that Ron Burckley had passed away, closing yet another chapter in the history of the old farmhouse. After the Schenck and the Mann families, the Burckleys lived there the longest. Ron's father, Raymond, had saved the house. Residing there between those hallowed walls on that stunning piece of land has been one of the most exceptional experiences of my life.

Nothing else happened that year on the restoration. Joel hurt his back—another setback. Between that and his ticker, he really had to take it easy. Emma Jane and Catharine Baldwin would just have to wait.

In the beginning of December, I was back in the Grand Canyon, this time with Bruce Oreck, Barack Obama's former ambassador to Finland. Bruce was a river guide in his youth, and after many attempts to hike the canyon together, we finally got a permit to hit the trail.

When I returned, Sandy had her third successful lung cancer surgery. Her surgeon, Dr. Raja Flores, is a genius. Among his other achievements, he had invented a procedure where he could operate on Sandy's lungs without cracking open her chest.

As much as I wanted to postpone my trip is as much as Sandy wanted me to go. I was such a royal pain to live with, she insisted. Flores raised his eyebrow at delaying the surgery. Wouldn't you? But he was okay with waiting a few more weeks for my return. He said, "This is an easy one."

The Burying Ground Preservation Group met once again at my house for our annual toast to the Schencks and each other. Kurt couldn't make it that January 6, due to family obligations, but Koli came instead. The first toast went to Joel, with best wishes for his health, and then to Kurt, who was with his mom. I wrote him afterward and assured him that when the project was over, we'd celebrate together.

By the end of April 2023, things were changing at the Sisters of Mercy. Mark Kurnicki asked me to see him. I went to his office, and he told me the girl's high school was going to close. He didn't know what was going on, other than he had to move. Mark handed me two large documents to have copied. The first was a rolled-up 1927 reproduction of the original 1893 survey of the Church land. Where the Schenck farmhouse is, it says "Land of George Mann."

The Schenck name appears only once on the entire map at the site we had been working on. I was so fascinated by the maps and the property owners' names that I didn't pay much attention to the word *Cemetery*, to the right of the words *Cemetery J. Schenck.* It was another triangle. The hypotenuse matched the Schenck side. The right angle was on the southeast. Completing the square. This had to be the Nostrand Family Burying Ground. How about that? Cemetery 104 was not one cemetery. It was two.

The second document was a July 5, 1955, survey of their land commissioned by the Convent of the Sisters of Mercy Brooklyn of Syosset, Town of Oyster Bay, Nassau County, New York. It has a large detail of the two cemeteries on it. These were some of the missing Church records that Stephen Cass couldn't find when his law firm did a title search for me 20 years earlier.

When Joel saw the 1955 survey, he said, "It shows there is a right of way from the road to the cemetery and that the Church has built a building across it." That building blocks not only access but also the view of the cemetery from the farmhouse. It also blocks it from the road, which may make it less vulnerable to vandalism than when it was sitting high on a hill for all to see. However, it sure exposes the scruples or, should I say, the lack thereof, of my neighbors. But there's more.

When I returned the documents to Mark, he told me the new administrator was walking around his office, saw the surveys, and told him to get rid of them. Once again I'm in Mark's debt for helping preserve history. The old surveys are now with the Oyster Bay Historical Society, in the possession of Zach and Kurt, and a PDF is with Barney at the library as well as Jeanne Gatto at Parks and Louis LaRusso with the Highway Department.

Mark told me he was having heart problems and needed an operation. Maybe that's what caused him to hand me those files. He had one other official document for me to see: the 1947 Raymond Burckley survey of my land. That's the one that shows the adjoining parcel to the east with the words "Land of Sisters of Mercy Convent (Set Aside in Perpetuity for Park Purposes)." I photographed the survey while I was in Mark's office. Seeing it rolled up with the other files told me the Church knew all along that trying to build a nursing home on this land would

All that's left of Phebe Jane McElroy, second wife of Henry Schenck.

Joel and his nephew Rocco, working on what I believe was Margaret, wife of John Marshall.

Coming down the home stretch. The bottom piece does not belong here. It could be the top left corner of one of the Simeons.

The ruins of one of the infant's markers. We'll never know whom it belonged to.

On Frost she's "Emma Jane Wanser, wife of Charles A. Wanser, daughter of James R. and Sarah (Schenck) Ellison, died January 15, 1870. Age 18 years." On DAR she's "Emma Jane Wouser (stone fallen)."

Tomb of an unknown child.

Catharine Baldwin, died September 3, 1854. Age 34 years. Hers was the last tablet to be erected.

Mark Kurnicki, Director of Maintenance, Sisters of Mercy, 1979–2024.

have been in violation of their covenants and restrictions. I'd call that a convenient reason for all their files to disappear.

Later that spring, Joel's back was feeling better, his heart was stable, and he returned to finish up the last of the work on May 23 and 24, 2023. This time he brought with him his young nephew Rocco. Rocco's name just didn't fit the part. But he, like his uncle and Zach, Kurt, and Koli can all look themselves in the mirror for the incredible things they've done. One of the last was finding the location for a large fragment I never thought we'd find a home for. It fit perfectly under the "roy" piece in the Phebe McElroy stone.

When Joel had some downtime, I mentioned to him that I'd driven past the Parsons Cemetery in Springs and lamented how beautiful it was compared to the Schencks'. "I wish this place looked like that," I said.

He replied, "I like this one better!"

With no fanfare, no heralding trumpets, no public officials or press, Joel and Rocco finally completed the last of the punch list for the Schenck Family Burying Ground restoration. Their work was finally over. And shortly after that, we all got a gut punch.

Kurt Kahofer fell seriously ill with cancer and had an extended stay in Stony Brook Hospital. How successful was his surgery and his chemotherapy? When Kurt read a draft of this manuscript he said to just write, "Doctor reports that Kurt is making their job easier."

There was a silver lining to the story. Due to everybody's availability, the wine tasting celebration went off on December 21, 2023, and Kurt was there with a great big happy smile on his face. I thanked the team for all their hard work, and we strolled over to take a look at what we had done:

32 marble headstones are all or partially repaired.

6 fieldstones, including the restored June 27, 1804, John Schenck marker, are standing upright.

1 decaying brownstone now has a few more pieces beside it.

24 footstones and one pallet with an assortment of broken stones are all at the site.

We ended the year closing the book on Cemetery 104.

Mark Kurnicki retired March 31, 2024, and moved to Vero Beach, Florida, with his wife, Barbara. Before he left, he brought over enough topsoil to level off the uneven ground that the Schenck family rests under.

The Burying Ground Preservation Group is still at it, saving other historic burying yards on Long Island. Koli got married. And Zach is using ground-penetrating radar, no less, at Sag Harbor's Old Burying Ground to locate the remains of an earthen British fort built there during the American Revolutionary War. Talk about another way to desecrate a cemetery! (Bring the equipment to Syosset when you're finished, Zach.)

Now I need to take a hike. I'm heading back to that big old hole in the ground in northern Arizona: the Grand Canyon. Otherwise, I'll be busy doing my "philanthropic work," picking up trash wherever I go. And every once in a while, I'll check in on the Schencks.

As to my wife, Sandy, well, she still loves me, but she still won't let me hold her hand.

Drone photo of the Schenck Family Burying Ground, facing east, February 2024.

The Garret Nostrand headstone is on the far right between the second and third rows.

Epilogue

Ground-Penetrating Radar reveals 82 graves in 7 to 10 rows

Of course, not being able to let it go, I went to Sag Harbor in the fall of 2024 to hunt down that GPR specialist. On June 27, 2025, Len Strozier arrived in Syosset. He explained that when a body decomposes, it leaves an air pocket he called a burial shaft. In the two cemeteries, Len discovered 82 burial shafts, 37 unmarked. He placed orange flags in the middle of each one and marked the length of all the departed with orange paint. He also circled 75 possible gravestone fragments.

It turns out none of the headstones we restored truly face east/west. They are off by about 10 degrees. Many aren't even over the graves. As to the rows, it's hard to get a count. They are oddly staggered, with irregular gaps between graves. The Nostrand Family side of the yard had dozens of people interred there, many of them children. Len's maps are in the Appendix.

Meet the last responder, Len Strozier.

I was given the assignment by Rav Freidel to scan this historic burial yard with Ground Penetrating Radar and capture my discovery with GPS. During the past 18 years I have walked hundreds of cemeteries across 25 states, from coastal burial grounds where sea winds weather burial stones rapidly, to isolated deep-wooded plots where slow-growing moss veils mostly-forgotten markers. Each cemetery has its own atmosphere, its own language, and its own contemplative hush. But I confess few stories have touched me more than these two graveyards in Syosset on Long Island.

It is difficult to write the next part, but honesty demands it. Multiple times in the twentieth century—no one seems to know the exact years—vandals entered this sacred space. The result was devastating. More than forty historic markers were smashed. Not toppled, not weather-worn, but pulverized. Think about that: over and over and over. What kind of soul raises a hammer to obliterate a name? To strike away the only record of a life lived? It is as if they believed memory itself could be killed and the stories beneath would vanish. For a time, a long time, it seemed they might be right. Where once there had been rows of names shining bright in the sun, then there were only piles of fragments, scattered across the ground.

Yes, this is where many histories vaporize. With silence. With rubble. With loss. But not here. Not this time. This is a story of resurrection. Like the mythical Phoenix rising from ashes, many of the Schenck headstones and at least one Nostrand headstone have been lifted, one by one, from heaps of rubble. They have been pieced together like fragile puzzles, their inscriptions coaxed back into legibility, their dignity restored, slowly and painstakingly. Imagine the patience: a hand lifting one shard, holding it against another, searching for a match. Imagine the hours comparing pieces, reading partial inscriptions, aligning edges.

I think of the devotion of Rav Freidel and his team bending in the grass, hands dirty with soil, eyes straining to read faint carvings. I think of the glue, the mortar, the metal braces that hold stones upright again.

That such a pure labor-of-love could happen in this twenty-first century—amid all our distractions, our screens, our noise—feels nothing short of miraculous. For this was not a government-funded restoration, not a corporate project. It was pure neighborly love.

And now many of the stones live again. And with them, the names of children, mothers, fathers, matriarchs and patriarchs, those whose dates stretch back to the earliest days of our nation.

I am honored to have been the last member of Rav's team of Cemeterians to give this ground a fresh voice—not only by recording what is visible, but by unveiling what was hidden.

What lessons does this offer us? That memory can be vanished only if we allow it. That heritage requires guardians. That cemeteries—those quiet corners in every community so easily overlooked—are not places of fear but of testimony. They remind us who we are, where we came from, what it costs for us to stand here today.

They hold up the truth that we too will pass. Silently asking what kind of a legacy will we leave? Will our deeds outlive us? Will our names be cherished? Will anyone bend to pick up the fragments of our story if it is ever shattered?

Respectfully,

Len Strozier
Omega Mapping Services
Columbus, Georgia
August 26, 2025

Len Strozier at the Old Burying Ground, Sag Harbor, New York October 17, 2024.

Orange flags mark the burial chambers of the obliterated Nostrand Family Burying Ground.

A 3-inch stainless steel disc has been placed in the center of each gravesite, marking the 82 graves in both cemeteries. The discs can be located with a metal detector.

"In this one extreme photo, we can see the cruelty of men versus the honor of men."
-Len Strozier, July 2025

JOHN SCHENCK
DIED
March 2, 1852,
Aged 77 Years.
7 Mo & 10 D's.

Appendix: Surveys and maps

1912 FROST SURVEY: *In 1902 John Wycoff visited the Schenck Family Cemetery. His field studies were transcribed by Josephine Frost. This is the earliest record of the interred, courtesy of the Brooklyn Historical Society.*

I N S C R I P T I O N S

F R O M

S C H E N C K C E M E T E R Y

A T

S Y O S S E T, L O N G I S L A N D

Schenck, James Henry Schenck, born Sep. 10, 1854, died Jan. 22, 1890

Schenck, Mary Eliza Schenck, born May 22, 1868, died April 8, 1897

Schenck, Ann E. Schenck, born April 25, 1870, died Aug. 17, 1870

Schenck, Elbert Schenck, born May 22, 1867, died Oct. 23, 1867

Schenck, Martha J. Schenck, born May 5, 1866, died July 23, 1866

Schenck, Nelson Schenck, born March 9, 1863, died July 27, 1863

Schenck, Jane E. Schenck, born Jan. 11, 1817, died March 16, 1858

Schenck, Henry Schenck, born July 3, 1817, died Dec. 16, 1873

McElvoy, Phebe Jane McElvoy, born July 25, 1841, died Jan. 25, 1890

Van Sise, Martha B. wife of Andrew Van Sise, born June 18, 1837, died April 29, 1864

Schenck, Martha, wife of Jacobus Schenck, born Oct. 21, 1793, died June 19, 1877

Schenck, Nelson Schenck, born March 6, 1833, died July 23, 1852

Schenck, Jacobus Schenck, born May 26, 1791, died Jan. 17, 1873

Schenck, Elbert Schenck, born Dec. 26, 1823, died June 23, 1845

Schenck, Mary Elizabeth Schenck, born Feb. 21,1819, died Jan. 21, 1890

Schenck, Simeon Schenck, born Oct. 12, 1815, died Oct. 11, 1880

Schenck, Juliette, daughter of Simeon and Mary Schenck, born Jan. 5, 1851, died Aug. 29, 1852

Schenck, Harriet A. daughter of Simeon and Mary Schenck, born Dec. 10, 1853, died Dec. 30, 1853

Schenck, Mary Emily, daughter of Simeon and Mary Schenck, born Sep. 27, 1844, died Feb. 16, 1854

Schenck, Jane, daughter of Simeon and Mary Schenck, born Feb. 12, 1854, died March 26, 1854

Schenck, Simeon, son of Simeon and Mary Schenck,born June 10, 1860, died Feb. 18, 1864

Schenck, Stephen Schenck, born March 29, 1824, died May 12, 1876

Schenck, Aaron Schenck, born Oct. 17, 1821, died March 3, 1863

Schenck, William Schenck, born Aug. 4, 1813, died Nov. 20, 1844

Schenck, John Schenck, born Aug. 17, 1808, died Mch. 4, 1838

Schenck, Jane Schenck, born Feb. 15, 1784, died Mch. 15, 1846

Schenck, Cornelia Schenck, born April 1, 1779, died July 5, 1855

Schenck, Stephen Schenck, born July 15, 1784, died Dec. 22, 1859

Ellison, Sarah, wife of James R. Ellison, born March 8, 1849, died Sep. 19, 1867

Ellison, Jane Louisa, daughter of James R. and Sarah Ellison, born April 29, 1851, died May 1, 1851

Wanser, Ellison, Emma Jane, daughter of James R. and Sarah Ellison and wife of Charles A. Wanser died Jan. 15, 1870. Age 18 years

Schenck, John Schenck, born July 20, 1774, died March 2, 1852

Schenck, Mary, wife of John Schenck, born Aug. 18, 1773, died Sep. 28, 1871

Schenck, Aaron Schenck, born Nov. 7, 1783, died Sep. 15, 1871

Schenck, Sarah, wife of Aaron Schenck, died Sep. 18 1880. Age 90 years

Marshall, Nicholas S. Marshall, born March 25, 1808, died June 30, 1875

Marshall, Schenck, Margaret, daughter of Nicholas and Catharine Schenck and wife of John Marshall born Aug. 5, 1786, died Oct. 9, 1821

Marshall, John Marshall, died Sep. 4, 1846. Age 71yrs

Lewis, Scudder Lewis, died July 15, 1849. Age 33ys

Lewis, Louisa Lewis, died March 10, 1854. Age12yrs

Baldwin, Catharine Baldwin, died Sep. 3, 1854. Age 34 years

C E M E T E R Y   I N S C R I P T I O N S

(Two miles from Hicksville, Long Island, on road leading to Syosset.)

Schenck, Nicholas Schenck, born Oct. 12, 1803, died Aug. 29, 1882

Schenck, Phebe Ann, wife of Nicholas Schenck, born May 8, 1807, died Feb. 8, 1895

Schenck, John J. son of Nicholas and Phebe Ann Schenck, born Feb. 13, 1845, died Oct. 20, 1877

Crooker, Rosetta Crooker, born Aug. 25, 1804, died July 6, 1883

1932 DAUGHTERS OF THE AMERICAN REVOLUTION (DAR) SURVEY:

The Daughters of the American Revolution (DAR) were the next to inventory the Schenck Family Burying Ground. Recorded in 1932 by the Ketewamoke Chapter of Huntington, Long Island, the names appear alphabetically. This is the only DAR survey of the site.

37

Schenck Burying Ground in Syosset on Old Schenck Farm on Nostrand Ave.
Town of Oyster Bay, Suffolk Co., N. Y.
(back of Catholic School-Sisters of Mercy Academy)

Baldwin, Catharine; d. Sept. 3, 1854. Ae. 34 yr.

Ellison, Sarah, wf. of James R. Ellison; d. Sept. 19, 1867. Ae. 48-6-14.
Ellison, Jane Louisa, dau. of James R. & Sarah Ellison; d. May 1, 1851. Ae. 2 da.

Lewis, Louise; d. Mar. 10, 1854. Ae. 12 yrs. (Stone fallen.)
Lewis, Scudder; d. July 5, 1849. Ae. 33 yr.

Marshall, John; d. Sept. 4, 1846. Ae. 71 yrs.
Marshall, Nicholas S.; d. June 30, 1875. Ae. 67-3-5.

Nostrand, Garret, d. July 10, 1843, in the 87th yr. of his age. Unmarked field stone beside it.

Schenck, Aaron; d. Mar. 3, 1863; Ae. 41-4-14. (Stone fallen.)
Schenck, Aaron; d. Feb. 15, 1871. Ae. 87-3-8.
Schenck, Sarah, wf. of Aaron Schenck; d. Sept. 18, 1880; Ae. 90 yr.
Schenck, Ann E. d. Aug. 17, 1870. A 3 mo. 23 d.
Schenck, Cornelius; d. July 5, 1855; Ae. 76-3-4.
Schenck, Elbert; d. June 23, 1845; Ae. 21-5-28.
Schenck, Elbert; d. Oct. 23, 1867; Ae. 5 mo. 1 d.
Schenck, Henry; d. Dec. 16, 1873; Ae. 56-5-13.
Schenck, Jacobus; d. Jan. 17, 1873; Ae. 81-7-22.
Schenck, Martha, wf. of Jacobus Schenck; d. June 19, 1877; Ae. 83-7-29.
Schenck, Jane; d. Mar. 15, 1846; Ae. 62 yr. 1 mo.
Schenck, Jane E.; d. May 16, 1858; Ae. 41-4-5.
Schenck, John; d. Mar. 4, 1838; Ae. 29-6-15.
Schenck, John; d. Mar. 2, 1852. Ae. 77-7-10.
Schenck, Mary, wf. of John Schenck; d. Sept. 28, 1871. Ae. 98-1-10.
Footstone L L with no headstone. Many field stone markers - no legible inscriptions.
Schenck, Martha J.; d. July 23, 1866; Ae. 5 mo. 18 d.
Schenck, Nelson; d. July 23, 1852; Ae. 19-2-7.
Schenck, Nelson A.; d. July 27, 1863; Ae. 4 mo. 18 d.
Schenck, Stephen; d. Dec. 22, 1859. Ae. 75-5-7.
Schenck, Stephen; d. May 12, 1876; Ae. 52-1-10.
Schenck, William; d. Nov. 20, 1844; Ae. 31-3-16.

Van Lise, Martha B., wf. of Andrew Van Lise; d. Ap. 29, 1864; Ae. 26-10-11.

Wouser, Emma Jane, wf. of Charles A. Wouser, dau. of James R. & Sarah Ellison; d. June 15, 1870. Ae. 18 yr. (Stone fallen.)

Copied Mar. 1, 1932 - G. G. Cockcroft.
Ketewamoke Chap.
Huntington, N.Y.

1940s BURCKLEY SURVEY: *This survey has been mistaken as a 1941 DAR survey. Raymond Burckley made this record c. 1945.*

Interments at the Schenck Cemetery
East Woods (Syosset) L.I.
Tombstone Inscriptions

Martha S, wife of Andrew Van Sise Died 3/29/1864, age 26 years 10 mos. and 11 days

Phebe Jane MacElroy, died 1/25/1890 [handwritten: 1890], 48 years 6 months

Jane M. Schenck, May 16, 1858, age 41 years 4 months, 5 days.

Henry Schenck died 12/16/1873, age 56 years 5 mos and 13 days.

Martha, wife of Jacobus Schenck died 6/19/1877, age 83 years, 7 mos. 29 days.

Jacobus ~~Schenck~~ Schenck (stone reads Chenck) died 1/17/1873, age 81 years, 7 mos and 22 days.

Nelson Schenck died 7/23/1852, age 19 years 2 mos, 7 days.

Elbert Schenck died 6/23/1815, age 21 years 5 mos and 28 days.

Mary Elizabeth Schenck died 1/21/1890, age 70 years 11 mos.

James Henry Schenck died 1/22/1890, age 35 years 4 mos and 12 days.

Mary Elizabether born 5/22/1868, died 4/~~1~~ 8/1897

2nd row

Stephen Schenck died 12/22/1859, age 75 years 5 mos and 7 days.

Cornelius Schenck died 7/6/1855 age 3 mos and 4 days.

James Schenck died 3/15/1846 age 62 years 4 mos.

John Schenck died 3/4/1838, age 29 years 6 mos and 15 days.

William Schenck died 11/20/1844, age 51 years 5 mos and 16 days.

Aron Schenck died 3/3/1863, age 41 years 4 mos and 14 days.

Stephen Schenck died 5/12/1876, age 52 years 1 mo and 13 days.

3rd row

Catherine Baldwin died Sept, 3, 1854 age 3 years.

Scudder Lewis died 7/15/1819 age 32 years.

John Marshall died 9/4/1846 age 71 years.

Stone Slab

Brown stone disfigured age 35 years.

LOCATED BEHIND SCHOOL DIRECTLY ACROSS. STREET

1962 VELSOR SURVEY: *The fourth documentation of the Schenck Burying Ground was performed by Dean Velsor in 1962 for the Town of Oyster Bay.*

The Schenck Cemetery. Located west of the St. Mary of the Angels Home on Convent Rd., Syosset. The cemetery is is poor shape. Two markers were lying face down and I was unable to lift them. Data collected by Dean H. Velsor on June 23, 1962.

Marker decorated with a hand pointing upwards;
Ane (or Ann),Louisa, dau. of James and Sarah Ellison, d. May 1st, 185(3?), Aged 2 days.

Sarah, wife of James R. Ellison, d. Sept. 19, 1867, Aged 48 (or 18)y. 6m. 11d.

Solitary, thick white stone;
In Memory of Garret Nostrand, who died July 1o, 1843 in the 87th year of his age.

Aaron Schenck, d. Mar. 3, 1863, Aged 41y. 4m. 14d.

In Memory of Aaron Schenck, d. Feb. 15, 1871, Aged 87y. 3m. 8d.

In Memory of Sarah, wife of Aaron Schenck, d. Sept. 18, 1880, Aged 90y.

Ann Schenck, d. Aug. 17, 187-, Aged 3m. 23d.

In Memory of Elbert Schenck, who died June 23, 1815, Aged 21y. 5m. 28d.

Henry Schenck, d. Dec. (17?), 1871, Aged 56y. 5m. 18d.

James Henry Schenck, d. Jan. 22, 1890, Aged 35y. 4m. 12d.

Jacobus Schenck, d. Jan. 187(7?), Aged 81y. 7m. 22d.

Martha, wife of Jacobus Schenck, d. June 19, 1877, Aged 83y. 7m. 29d.

Jane Schenck, d. Mar. 15, 1846, Aged 62y. 1m.

Jane Schenck, d. May.16, 1858, Aged 41y. 4m. 5d.

John Schenck, d. Mar. 2, 1852, Aged 77y. 7m. 10(?)d.
Martha J. Schenck, d. July 23, 1866, Aged 5m. 18d.

Mary Elizabeth Schenck, d. Jan. 21, 1890, Aged 7y. 11m.

In Memory of Nelson Schenck, who died July 23, 1855,
Aged 19y. 2m. 7d.

Stephen Schenck, d. May 12, 1876, Aged 52y. 1m. 13d.

Martha, Wife of Andrew Van Sise, d. Apr. 29, 1861, Aged
26y. 10m. 11d.

There is one red sandstone marker in the cemetery. It is completely eroded and faceless.

3 or 4 plain fieldstone markers.

Syosset

(104) Schenck Family Cemetery

West of Our Lady of the Angels Home, approx. 300 ft north of Convent Road.

Inscriptions-Frost 1912; DAR 1941: TOB June 23, 1962 plus additions Dec. 3, 1975.

Schenck, Ann (Inf) 187_ 104

Schenck, Aaron 1863 104

Schenck Aaron 1871 104

Schenck Cornelius 1855 104

Schenck, Elbert 1815 104

Schenck, Henry 1890 104

Schenck, Jacobus 1877 104

Schenck, James Henry 1890 104

Schenck, Jane 1846 104

Schenck, Jane 1858 104

Schenck, John 1838 104

Schenck, John 1852 104

Schenck, Martha 1877 104

Schenck, Martha J. 1866 104

Schenck, Mary 1871 104

Schenck, Mary Eliza 1897 104

Schenck, Mary Elizabeth 1890 104

Schenck, Sarah 1880 104

Schenck, Stephen 1859 104

Schenck, Stephen 1876 104

Schenck, William 1844 104

RE-CREATION OF THE PEOPLELEGACY.COM SURVEY: *This survey was discovered by Kurt Kahofer on the Internet. We have no idea when it was compiled or by whom.*

Mary Eliza Schenck: Died 1897

Mary Elizabeth Schenck: Died 1890

James Henry Schenck: Died 1890

Henry Schenck: Died 1890

Simeon Schenck: 1815-1880 (aged 65)

Sarah Schenck: Died 1880

Martha Schenck: Died 1877

Jacobus Schenck: Died 1877

Stephen Schenck: Died 1876

Mary Schenck: Died 1871

Aaron Schenck: Died 1871

Emma Jane Ellison Wansor 1852-1870 (aged 18)

Ann Schenck: Died 1870

Sarah Schenck Ellison: Died 1867 Born in Oyster Bay, NY

Martha J Schenck: Died 1866

Martha Boerum Schenck Van Sise 1837-1864 (aged 26)

Aaron Schenck: Died 1863

Steven Schenck: Died 1859

Jane Schenck: Died 1858

Cornelius Schenck: Died 1855

Nelson Schenck: 1833-1852 (aged 19)

John Schenck: Died 1852

Jane Louisa Ellison: 1851-1851 (aged less than a year)

Jane Schenck: Died 1846

William Schenck: Died 1844

John Schenck: Died 1838

Elbert Schenck: Died 1815

***1927 COPY OF 1893 CONVENT OF THE SISTERS OF MERCY MAP:** In 1893, the Sisters of Mercy bought the land where the Schenck family is laid to rest. A portion of the 1927 reproduction of their original map shows the cemetery (see insert). It's the only mention of the Schenck name on the map.*

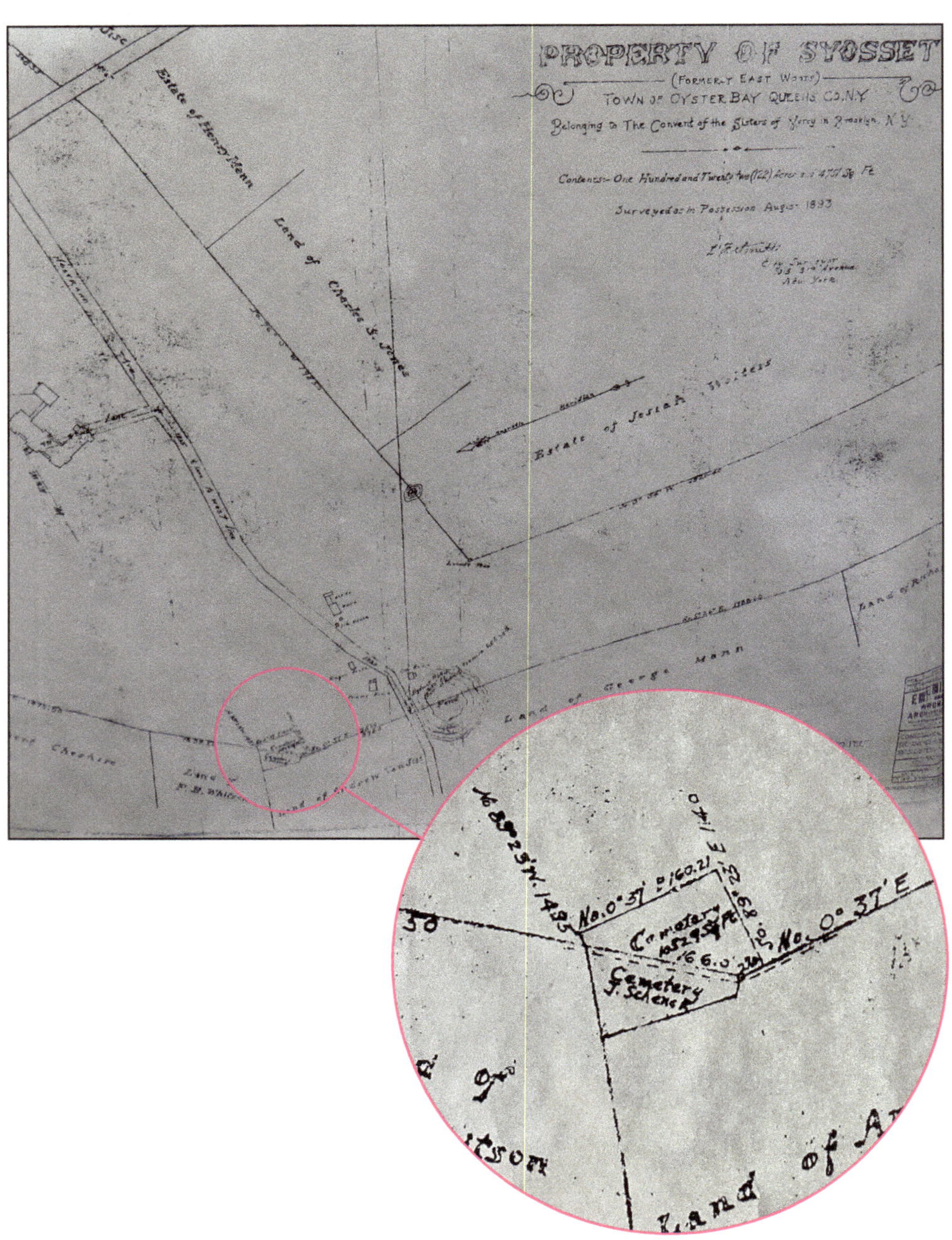

1955 CONVENT OF THE SISTERS OF MERCY MAP: *In the lower right is an inset of the two cemeteries: "Cemetery J. Schenck" and "Cemetery." I had wondered if the one marked "Cemetery" on the 1893 map was the missing Nostrand family site. They owned the land before the Church bought it. Indeed, it was.*

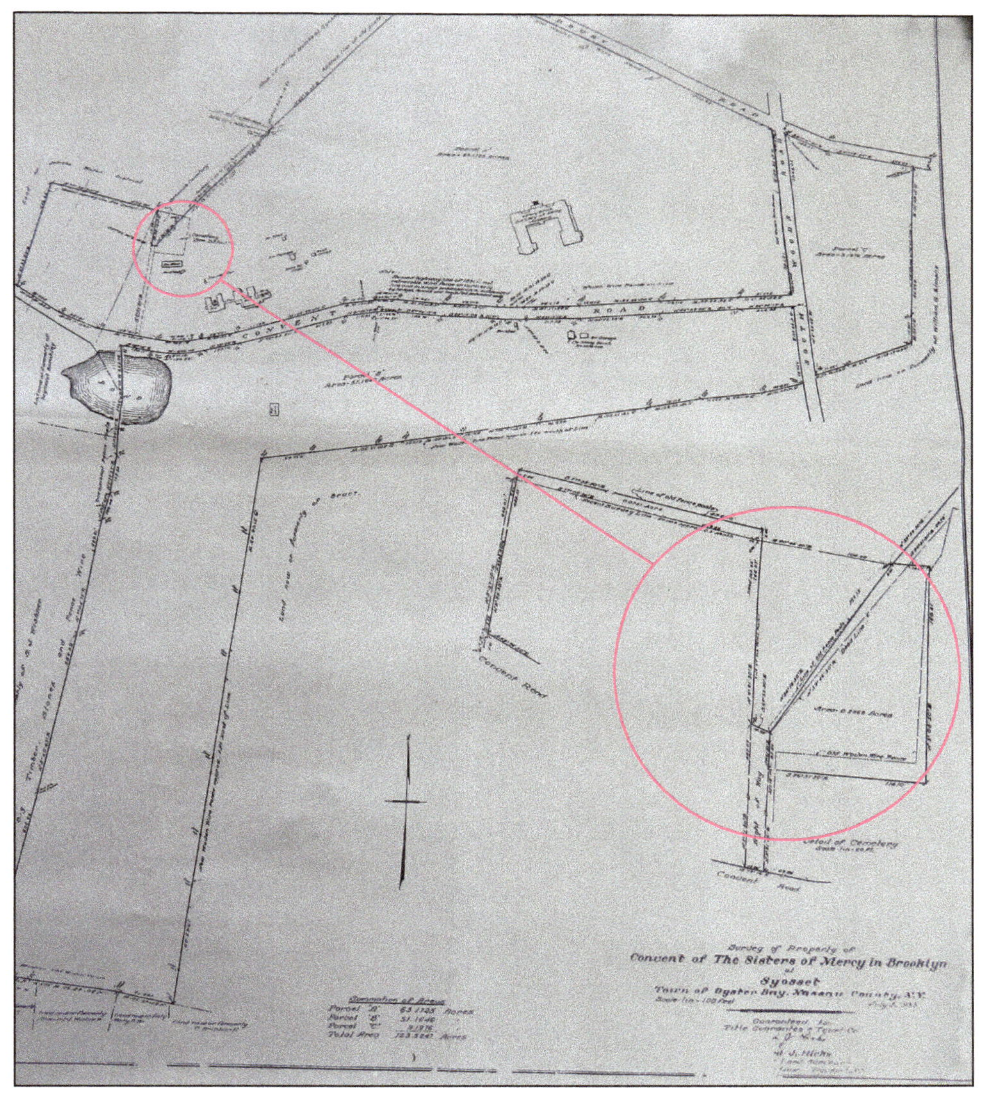

***1947 RAYMOND BURCKLEY MAP OF THE SCHENCK-MANN FARM-HOUSE AND LAND:** This map is in the possession of the Sisters of Mercy and photographed with Mark Kurnicki's assistance. Note the wording on the right side of the map: "Land of Sisters of Mercy Convent (Set aside in perpetuity for park purposes)." I hope they honor this.*

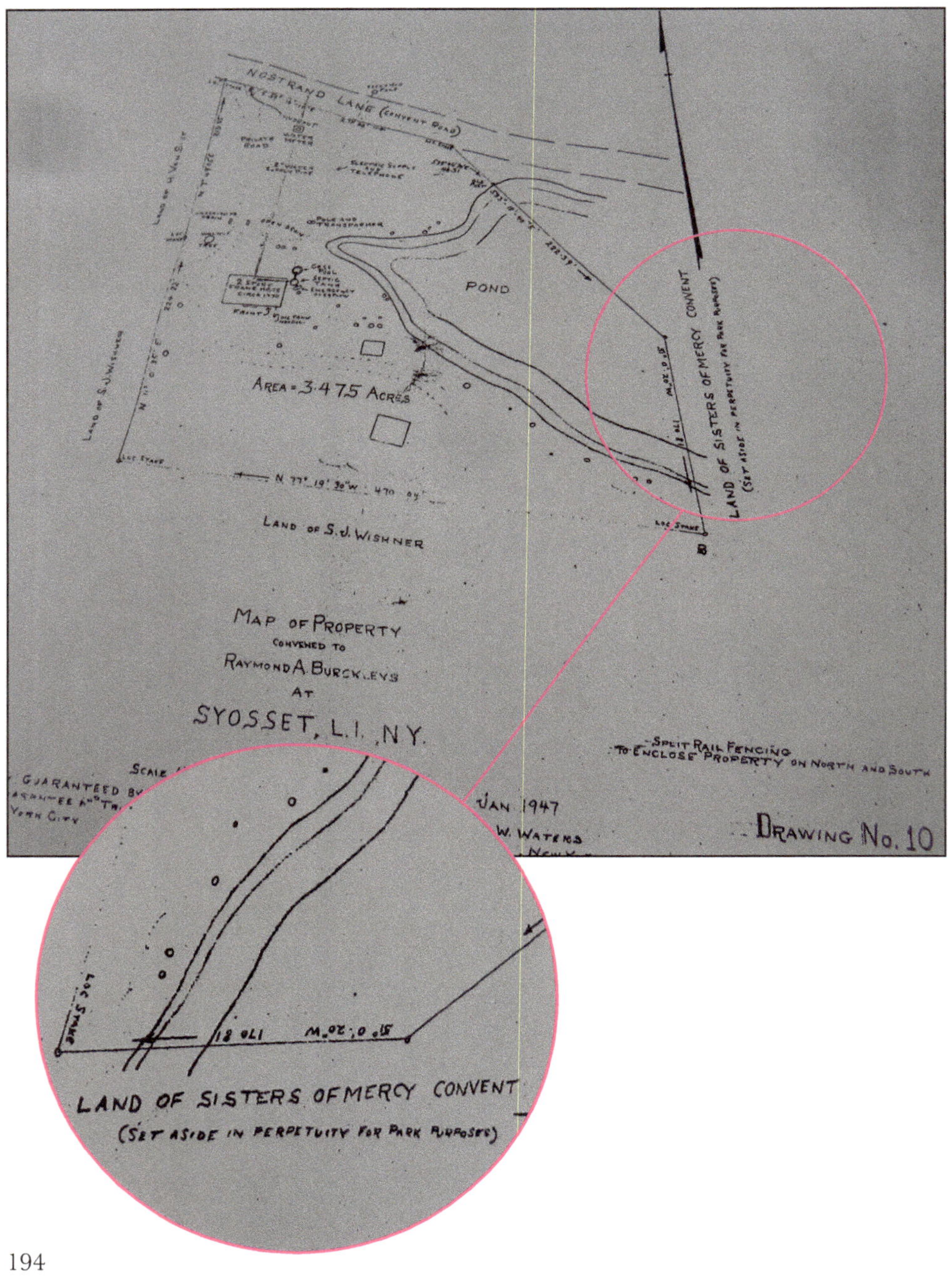

1873 SYOSSET/WOODBURY MAP: *This was hanging in Mark Kurnicki's office. He gave it to me before he moved away. It's the earliest record of where everybody lived.*

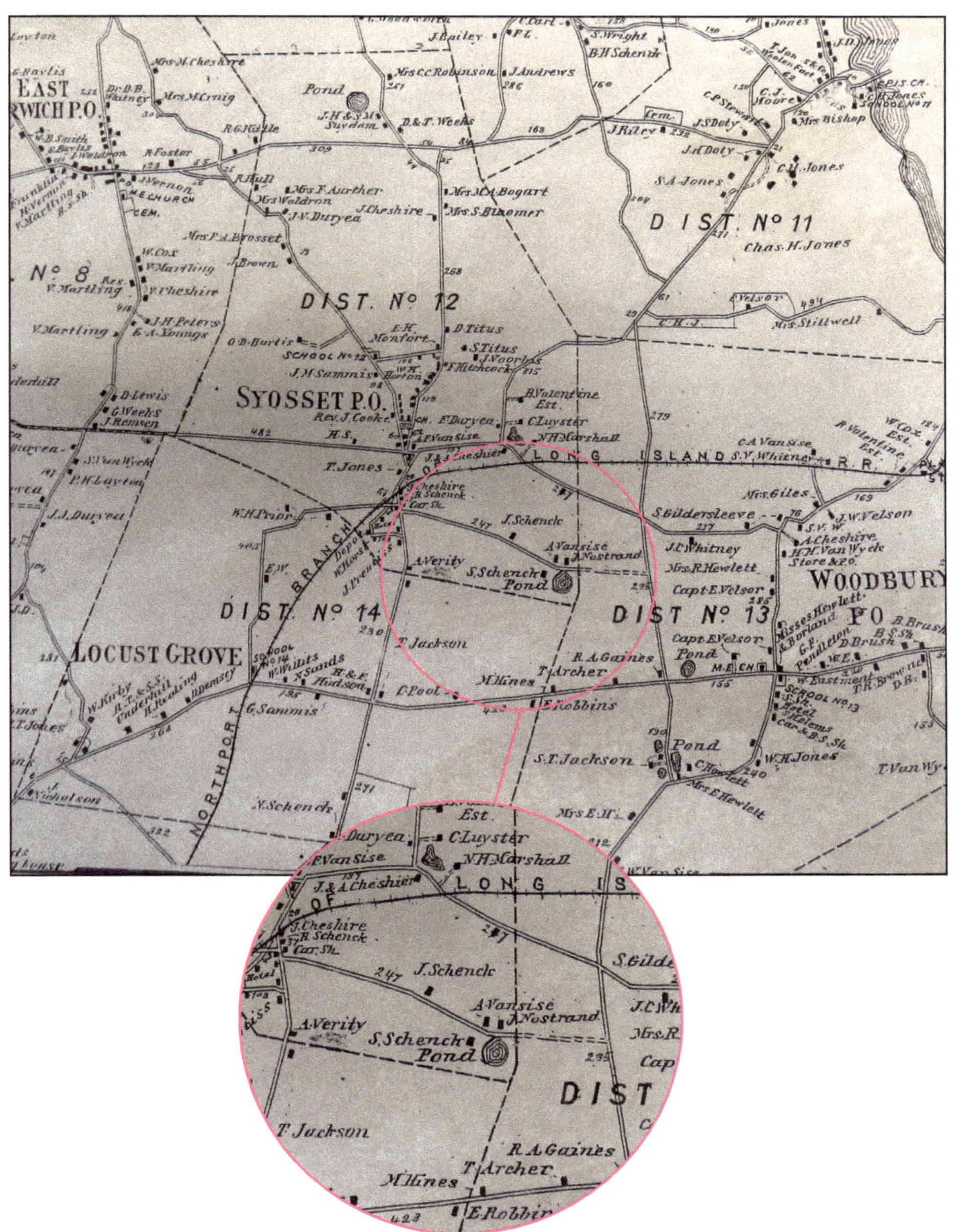

OMEGA MAPPING SERVICES: *Grave depictions by Len Strozier, July 27, 2025, show 82 burial shafts covering both burying grounds.*

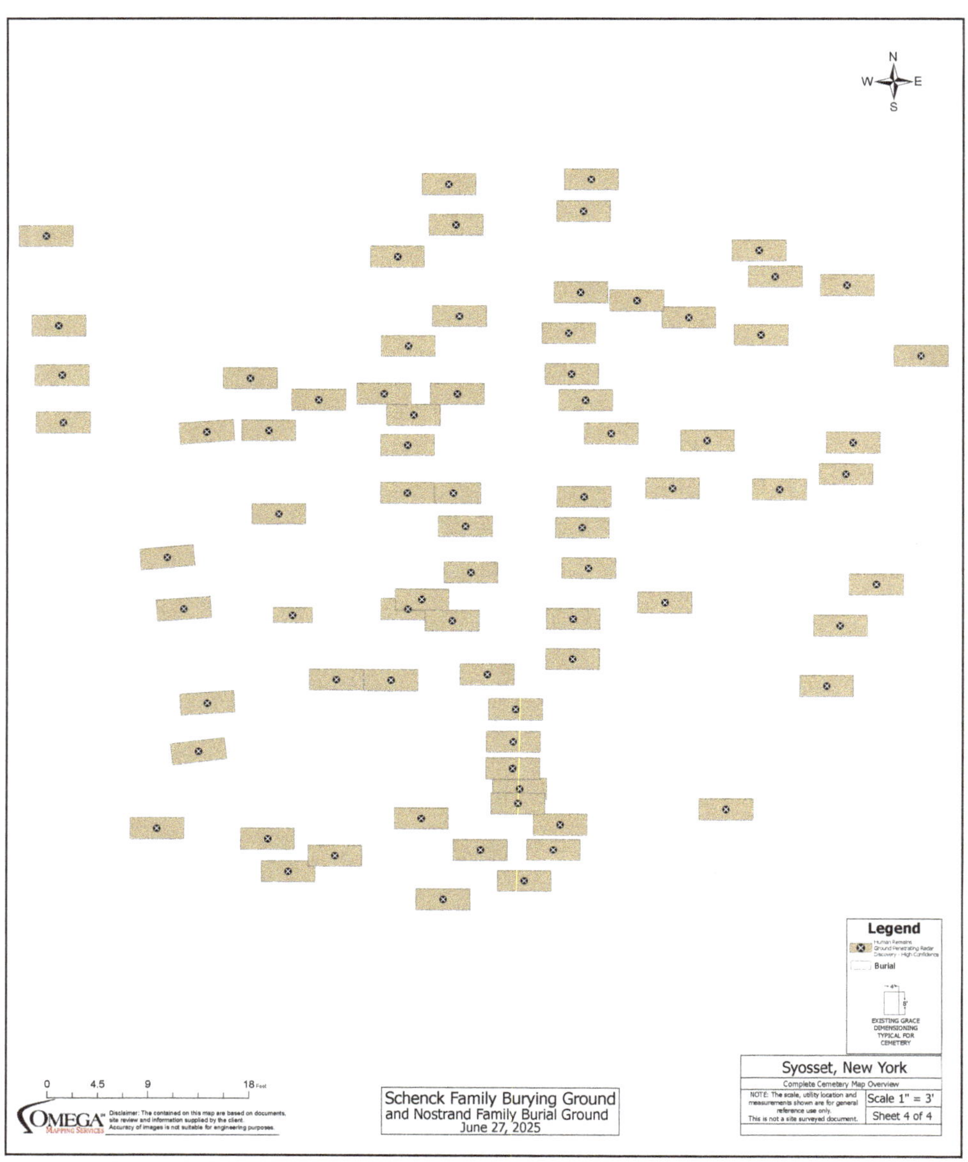

OMEGA MAPPING SERVICES: *Len Strozier map shows an overlay of both the restored headstones and the actual burial sites. The three unknown boxes to the east are large rocks and not memorials.*

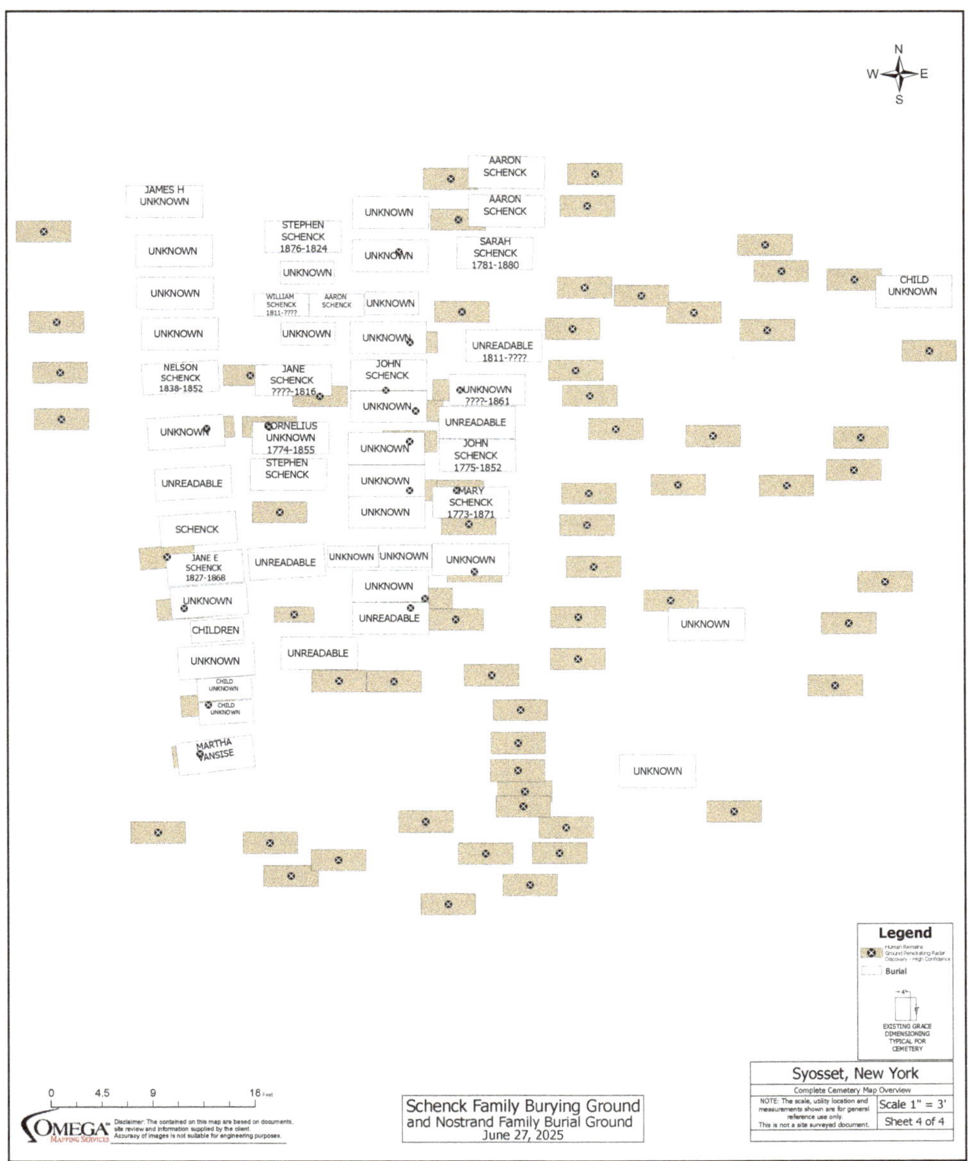

These remaining fragments (now wrapped in geotextile material and buried three paces northeast where they appear in the aerial photograph on page 175) await a future restoration effort.

Acknowledgments

I had no intention of writing a book about the final resting place of anyone, let alone the people who built and lived in my house starting 300 years ago. What I wanted to do was update the survey. However, too many headstones are in the wrong places. Too many educated guesses took place in figuring out who's who and what's what. And they're just guesses. Plus, so much is no longer there. Or if it is, I haven't found it yet. These pages seemed like the best way to bring everything up to date and to both memorialize and thank everybody who helped save this small part of history.

There are some others involved in this undertaking whose names haven't been mentioned. They were every bit as valuable. A special thank you goes to my art director, Jill Fleming, who turned my manuscript and a bunch of pictures in a Word document into something I would want to read. You've got a great eye and great sense of design, my friend. And you're a damn good writer, too.

Jill and I were aided in this undertaking by my incredible copyeditor/proofreader, Eva Langfeldt. She is the goods. I was introduced to her by a writer I never met, Mike Dillon, a friend of Bill Hoke. Mike said, "Proofreaders have gone the way of the buffalo hunter." Thank you, Mike. I am incredibly lucky to have had Eva working on this. She caught a staggering number of mistakes. I'm in awe of her talent and editing skills.

One more person needs to be thanked, again: my old friend Don Wood. Although he's in the story, after he read the manuscript, he sent me *The Art of Readable Writing*, by Rudolf Flesch. It was written when I was 2. The crux of it was something an old advertising legend, Ed McCabe, used to scream in my ear. "Never use a two-syllable word when you can use one. Make it so the doorman can understand it and the taxi driver can understand it. The Ph.D. will understand it, too!"

www.ingramcontent.com/pod-product-compliance
Lightning Source LLC
LaVergne TN
LVHW052353100826
845147LV00013B/825
* 9 7 9 8 2 1 8 8 4 1 8 7 4 *